Designed for Success

A FRESH LOOK AT THE BIRTH AND THE STAYING POWER OF THE CHURCH

Nathan Strong

ISBN: 1507612117
ISBN 13: 9781507612118
Library of Congress Control Number: 2015900890
CreateSpace Independent Publishing Platform
North Charleston, South Carolina

Available at Amazon.com
Wholesale at www.jessestrong.com

Designed for Success

Also by Nathan Strong
Available at Amazon.com

Thoughts for Jesse
A Father's Tribute

Before he was deployed to Iraq, Marine Sgt. Jesse Strong gave his minister/ author dad a list of theological/life questions to answer for him in writing. When Jesse was killed while on patrol, his father set out to answer those questions for him, in his memory. The resulting book has been appreciated by others considering answers to similar questions.

What reviewers on Amazon are saying about **Thoughts for Jesse:**

"Wonderful, insightful book. This book is on the level of "Radical" by Platt and many of the other current books that so eloquently help us better understand the Bible and its relevance to a 21st century Christian in America."

"Great 'How to' book. This book has all the important everyday answers to most all basic failures that are so common in today's society."

"A wonderful book about a wonderful young man."

This book is designed as supplemental reading for any study of church planting, church growth, the early church or the Book of Acts.

It can be used as a ten week Bible study as it has discussion questions after each chapter.

It is also profitable as an encouraging fresh look at the birth and the staying power of the church and how we can be part of God's continuing plan.

For Vicki, my wife
Friend and confidante extraordinaire

"...heirs together of the grace of life"

Author's Note

From my earliest days as a Christian, I have wrestled with the concept of the church's responsibility to take the Gospel to the world and struggled with my guilt when I hear missionary speakers say things like, "People are still waiting after 2000 years!" Was the task given to the twelve disciples actually mission impossible? Was Jesus setting them up for failure?

Then I read again two of Jesus' parables – the ones about the kingdom of heaven being like leaven or a mustard seed – and realized that Jesus set them up for success, not failure. Just as the leaven can't help but leaven the whole, and the mustard seed can't help but grow big, even so the church was designed for success! It was designed by God Himself to take the good news to the whole world during each generation, and it has, even though there are always unreached pockets. Come with me and explore the amazing phenomenon which is the church.

Table of Contents

INTRODUCTION   CONTINUITY

"We have this treasure in earthen vessels, that the excellence of the power may be of God and not of us." - 2 Corinthians 4:7

n 1961, Bruce Olson, a young American missionary, with no more training than his own deeply personal relationship with Jesus and some refined linguistic skills, wandered into contact with a stone age jungle tribe in South America. Learning their language and their culture as he relied on their hospitality, he eventually was able to introduce them to Jesus in a way they could comprehend, and they embraced the living Saviour for themselves. Thus was born the Motilone church, a vibrant, self-sustaining, self-propagating branch of the body of Christ which brought communion with God to the tribe and the life-giving Gospel to its neighbors.

The original church-planting model proved its effectiveness once again, after two thousand years, in a place with no contact with the Gospel until that young missionary joined their tribe. An introduction to a personal relationship with Jesus in a way people can understand, by a person who knows the Saviour personally, continues to produce the fruit of the Vine, as it has since Pentecost. Sharing something as deep and personal as unity with Jesus and communion with God will always produce self-sustaining life. Anything less is mere proselytizing.

The challenge involved in such a scenario was summed up succinctly in an introduction to a television series about Christianity – "How did a despised religion of outcasts and slaves survive and thrive?" And I'm sure the "renowned scholars, thinkers, and artists" featured in the series did their best to plumb the depths of history, demographics, and human tendencies in seeking the answer to that question. But that question cannot be answered through that means, despite our very human confidence to the contrary.

For years I have been a student of the early church and subsequent church planting, maintenance and growth. I studied it in college and through the years since. I've been personally involved in it during thirty years of pastoral ministry. However, I have always looked at it from the human perspective – how did *we* do it – Paul's missionary journeys, the work of other apostles, the follow up epistles, the modern missionary movement, contemporary church growth, etc.

For me, that perspective changed recently. I was working my way through the Book of Acts and the Epistles of Paul again and began to notice and concentrate on something different. Paul was so focused on God's part of the endeavor and what He was doing through weak human instruments that it made me turn my attention in that direction, as well. Paul was concerned that "the excellency of the power may be of God, and not of us." It was his concern with God's part which made his part what it ought to be.

By focusing on the human perspective it seemed like we were missing the most important element of the early church. It struck me that we really needed to consider the story of how *God* planted *His* church in such a way that it would thrive and grow until Christ's return. Paul saw this as the key, and it seemed like this should be our focus, too.

I became fascinated by this approach and became absorbed in the wonder of what God was doing in the world through "earthen vessels" empowered by the Holy Spirit to plant a church which would not only survive in hostile territory, but could reproduce itself without diminishing the force of the Gospel, and could reach the world with the good news of redemption. It seemed to me that there was much to be learned about how He did it which would apply directly to our church planting and growing attempts. He doesn't change, and the methods He employed successfully at the beginning of the church age should be helpful as we near the end of the age.

Ironically, I have been to church growth seminars and have heard of others and have never heard about this. I have heard about what Rick Warren is doing at Saddleback. I have heard about what Schuler did at the Crystal Cathedral. I heard about what they are doing at Willow Creek. I heard Dr. Paul Yongi Cho explain what he was doing at his 100,000 member church in Korea, the largest church in the world. But I have never, not once, heard about what Jesus did with His church. There is something strange and vaguely disturbing about that.

Therefore, this book does not attempt to be an exposition on church growth, as we have come to expect in our modern age. Rather, it is an exploration of how God brought the church into being and nurtured it, so that it was not only sustainable, but would flourish for two thousand years. Not designed as an exhaustive study, it brings a fresh perspective which hopefully will pique your interest in God's approach to the church. It's a starting point for what I hope will be your further study into God's plan and power for the church. I hope you find it fascinating, as well, and helpful in empowering you for the part God has given you to play in His church.

CHAPTER 1   FOUNDATION

"The foundation of God stands sure, having this seal, the Lord knows those who are His." - 2 Timothy 2:19

When Jesus came to earth 2000 years ago, we know He came to teach, to help and heal, and to die and rise again to redeem a fallen world. What we often overlook, however, is that He also came to lay the foundation for the church, a foundation which would sustain it until He came again. It was going to have to be a good foundation if He was going to go back to His Father and leave the church in the hands of His disciples. You'd think He would have spend a lot of time and effort teaching and training His disciples in church planting skills, but He didn't. He spent most of His time building a personal relationship with them; and then He simply told them to go and tell others the good news of redemption.

This begs the question, "What kind of foundation is that?" And if this is the foundation which would carry the church for 2000 years, perhaps we should examine it more closely. This foundation implies something other than human strategy and effort as the basis for church planting, maintenance and growth. Understanding this foundation should help us as we seek to carry on the work of the church today.

To start a book about how God planted and sustained His church, we must begin where He did, with His basic underlying concept. Paul, one of the original co-laborers in God's church planting project, said the foundation was that God knows those who are His. This may seem to lead to a discussion about foreknowledge as opposed to predestination, or vice versa, but not here. Here, we merely deal with the main, inescapable thought that God knows those who are His. This assumption changes everything about how we understand and plan and participate in church planting and growth.

Jesus said it in a very powerful way when He said, "Lift up your eyes, and look on the fields; for they are white already for harvest." And He said this in a "closed country" – Samaria – where the disciples wouldn't even consider sharing the Gospel, knowing two certain things, the Samaritans wouldn't listen, and they probably didn't deserve to hear. But Jesus knew that there were those who were His in this closed and disdained land, and He was already reaching out to them.

And, wonder of wonders, they were responding – first, the woman at the well and then "many more" from the city because of her testimony and then the personal teaching of Jesus. The disciples were astounded that the opportunity for forgiveness and fellowship with God, which they were only just beginning to understand, was available to the Samaritans, as well. How we need a similar attitude adjustment, which is what an understanding of the foundation can do, if we are "hearing".

■ ■ ■

The Creator, Who planned a wonderful life for us on a beautiful earth, also planned a means of worldwide and on-going redemption after we made a mess of things; and that plan included the church, planned in and through Christ before the world began. He always fulfils His plans and invites us to be a participant in them, if we like. However, it's His plan, completed at His initiative and by His power; and we would do well to understand it and volunteer to be part of it, rather than trying to accomplish it ourselves. It's His harvest. We are just the workers, co-laborers by His grace.

Jesus came to call and prepare volunteers for that plan who could go and replicate the process, even as He was paying the price for that plan to work. He obviously did not come to teach people how to be church planters. If that was the case, He would have taught more church growth seminars as we see them today. Instead, He called His disciples into a personal relationship with Himself and taught them how to become involved in God's plan and power. He understood the underlying concept and how people would fit into it. The result was so revolutionary that we really can't understand it without close scrutiny, and when we do look close, we have a hard time believing it.

It has always amazed me how He sent out the first twelve and then seventy, "as sheep among wolves." This was early in His ministry, when His disciples knew hardly more than that the Messiah had come and had the power to do a few miracles. He gave them extraordinary authority and responsibility as amateurs who barely understood what was going on. He sent them around the country, telling them to heal and to cast out demons themselves and to preach that the kingdom of heaven was at hand. And they went and did just that, ordinary people with no more training than time with and simple observation of Jesus.

They came back with joy, amazed that "it worked!" – people were healed and demons were cast out – just because they were obedient volunteers in God's plan. For some reason, we never stop to consider how unlikely that was. We simply take it for granted as part of the Gospel story. How did beginners with so little understanding of the concept or how it worked accomplish so much, simply by obeying the Master? The conclusion is inescapable – being part of the plan works, no matter who you are or what training you have.

I have tried this. Perhaps you have, as well. In my youthful, enthusiastic, newly Christian days I wanted to experience what these early disciples did. With probably more "witnessing" training than they had, I went out into the world to share the Gospel. However, my experience was nothing like theirs, despite my training and enthusiasm. I saw no healings or demons cast out. And, though I experienced His grace for my efforts, very few people found Christ through my preaching on street corners or in local parks.

I assumed I must be missing something and could not comprehend how this seemingly Biblical method would ever reach my neighborhood, much less the world. Since then I have been involved in ministry in many ways and have seen many come to Christ, but have only begun to understand the original problem as I researched this book. A better understanding of the foundation – the Lord knows those who are His – has helped and has also explained my "success" in the meantime. It's His plan and purpose, not my enthusiasm and efforts, which reaches the world. He knows who, what, where and when, and by His grace and power, He knows how and how I can be involved.

■ ■ ■

Let's examine this foundation – the Lord knows those who are His. It's obvious, regardless of your theology, that God knows those who are interested in, perhaps even waiting for, the Gospel in every country, culture, language and people group. Understanding this principle, Paul sought those people out in each city; shared the Gospel with them in a way they could understand; gave them the basics of a relationship with Jesus; made sure "it took"; then left them in God's hands as he went on to the next city, following up with them through the mail and through other co-laborers.

Oops! I just told you the whole book in one Paul-style sentence. Oh well, perhaps that will pique your interest in the details, which are so different from our contemporary approaches. God is up to something big, something wonderful, a way to reach the world with the good news. He has a big plan, has been working it for 2000 years, and offers us the chance to be part of it.

If this is true, we don't need to come up with our own plan. We don't need to drum up interest in the Gospel or try to "sell" Jesus, as though He were a product which we must convince others that they need. We must simply get the needed information to those who are waiting to hear it in a way they can understand it. And we begin with the knowledge that God has prepared the way, and the Holy Spirit is ready to empower us to do our part.

We don't have to develop strategies or organize institutions for church planting. We don't have to study demographics or the psychology or sociology of religion to reach people for Christ. It's a "God thing", and we must learn how to be a part of that.

He's been planning the church since before the beginning. He laid the groundwork for it before Jesus came. He paid for it in the death and resurrection of the Savior. He provided the power for it in the gift of the Holy Spirit and in the gifts of the Holy Spirit. He has gifted people to fill positions to hold it together and carry it forward. He takes "outcasts and slaves", fishermen and tax collectors, along with the occasional doctor, lawyer or Pharisee and calls them into a personal relationship with Jesus, God in the flesh, Someone they can understand and know. He then blends them in divine fellowship, and, "voila!", the church is born and flourishes for 2000 years, bringing hope, redemption and life to this tired old world, despite human foibles and failures which threaten to undermine and even to destroy the church which looks so vulnerable at first glance.

Jesus said the fields are white already for harvest. He also said that the Son of Man would be rejected, suffer and die and rise again. In other words, people are waiting, but not everyone is interested. Jesus also said that we can expect the same response that He received – some would listen, and some would reject Him. Therefore, our efforts are to be based in God's leading, rather than in perceived results. And He reminds us over and over that it's His church, that Jesus is the Head of it, and that we are merely branches on the Vine, totally dependent upon Him for guidance and strength as co-laborers in His harvest.

■ ■ ■

Reading in Joshua this morning, I came to a passage where one tribe was complaining about the land given to them by lot by Joshua. After saying it was too small, they went on to say that it would be too hard to conquer, as the inhabitants had iron chariots. After I finished mentally mocking them for their lack of faith – God miraculously brought them out of Egypt, parted the Red Sea and the Jordan River, and knocked down the walls of Jericho, and they're worried about "too hard" – I began to consider our view of church planting in difficult countries. We talk about "closed" countries where it is too hard, and they have cultures of iron, and we ignore the foundation.

"Too hard" is not a factor when the Lord is involved, when He knows the situation and knows those who are His. Just as He did with the children of Israel going into the Promised Land, conquering peoples and cities too strong for them, so he can do and has done with us, planting and sustaining His church in open and closed countries. We need the same attitude that He expected from the children of Israel – nothing is too hard, no countries are "closed" – if we follow His plan and walk in His power, giving Him a chance to share the Gospel through us with those who are His.

A case in point: the ancient city of Corinth, one of Paul's longer church planting stops. Here he worked with Aquila and Priscilla making tents, discipling this couple and preaching the Gospel to both Jews and Greeks. Although he faced persecution here, he stayed for a year and a half, operating under a direct word from the Lord, "I have many people in this city." The Lord knew those who were His and protected Paul until they each had a chance to hear. This is the kind of foundation of encouragement that we need as we seek to do our part in the plan.

Another, modern, case in point: the "closed country" of Iraq. Different missionaries had labored there for years, with seemingly little results. Then God took a hand in His time and way, although I wouldn't dare try to explain why or what the theological implications were. All I know is that after the war in Iraq began, Campus Crusade alone began to receive 16,000 inquiries *every day* at their evangelism centers in Iraq. God knows those who are His, and He found a way to get the Gospel to them when they were ready to respond.

The foundation is sure. It held the early church as it was beginning. It has carried the church through trials and tribulations. It has preserved the character of the church through centuries of heresies and doctrinal attacks; so the basic church is the same as the one

Jesus bought and paid for, and it continues with the same force and power to redeem, despite repeated attempts to take it in different directions.

This is amazing! It is well worth a television series to examine how it could possibly have happened. However, the only reason it could have happened is because the foundation is sure. We would do well to examine, understand and apply this underlying concept if we want to be part of the living, enduring church today as God continues to use it to bless a needy world.

Discussion questions:

1. What kind of foundation did Jesus lay for the church, and why?
2. What kind of foundation had God built into His world which made Jesus' foundation viable, making it possible for Jesus to send out disciples as "sheep among wolves"?
3. Why don't we have to develop strategies or organize institutions for church planting? What is the alternative?
4. What are the two sides of the "the servant is not greater than his Lord" coin (John 15:20)? How does this direct and encourage us?
5. How should we deal with the "it's too hard" problem of church planting?

CHAPTER 2   PROPHECY

"Look to Me, and be saved, all you ends of the earth!
For I am God, and there is no other." - Isaiah 45:22

Since God has been planning the church around Christ's coming since before the world began, it's obvious that He could reveal His strategy through prophecy, which begins to give us insight into His plan for the world and for the church which will carry out that plan. Although God uses Jewish channels to disclose His vision, we see a twofold purpose whenever we see prophecy about Messiah's coming – one for Israel and one for the rest of the world. God has a heart for His chosen people *and* for all other people yet to hear. This is plain throughout the Bible, and it will help us understand the big picture as we begin to examine the birth of the church.

In Isaiah 49, the prophet speaks of Messiah coming to begin the work of restoring Israel, but he goes on to say that He will also be "for a light to the Gentiles, that He may be My salvation unto the end of the earth." This theme is a constant in prophecy in many places and in different ways. Gentiles enter into prophecy just as Israel does, and for the same reason – God's love for people covers all people, and His plan for the church is about a *worldwide* church. Is it any wonder that the great commission is almost a direct quote of this prophecy?

Isaiah 60 says that the Gentiles will come to the Light which will come and kings (nations) to the brightness of His coming. This implies that the message of the Saviour will go to the whole world. It also implies that all nations and peoples will be involved in the Church, as they respond to the Light. As the Lord tells us about the Light Who will come to His people Israel, He also lays out His plan for a global community of believers.

Daniel 7:14 tells how dominion and glory and a kingdom will be given unto the Son of Man, and all peoples, nations and languages will serve Him. What a wonderful picture of the fulfillment of the Abrahamic covenant – that the whole world will be blessed through the Seed of Abraham. It's also a wonderful picture of the international church serving the King of kings, the Redeemer come for all mankind, the Father's intent from the beginning and one which He will carry out. This is a clear delineation for Israel and for us that Messiah comes to be the Savior of the world, not just a small part of it.

Hosea 2:23 speaks of how the Lord will have mercy on those who had not obtained mercy; will say to those who were not His people, "You are my people!" and they will say, "You are my God!" Peter, the apostle who had much prejudice about the Gentiles, quotes this passage referring to Gentiles who had become part of the church. Whether he thought this referred to backslidden Jews or to peoples outside his nation, it was clear that he saw the church including a wider range of people than he had first thought. This was God's plan from the beginning. How we need a wider vision, as well, seeing people we may ignore, seeing them as people God wants to make part of His people, part of His priesthood, part of His chosen generation.

Malachi 1:11 tells how the Lord's name will be great among the Gentiles of all nations around the world – from the rising of the sun to its going down. God sent His Son to live among His chosen people, fulfilling His promise to David; but when Jesus went to the cross of Golgotha, just outside of Jerusalem, He died and rose again for the whole world. Jesus could easily have been referring to this prophecy after His resurrection when He told His disciples to go into the world and preach the Gospel to everyone. As Malachi was the final Word from God before the four hundred silent years, the Jews would have studied this carefully, looking for Elijah's return; and they would have read over and over again that the Gentiles would be included in God's plan for the future.

And then there's the last minute prophecy, or, technically, the first minute prophecy, from the first few days of Jesus' earthly life – Simeon. He sums up all the other prophecies and says the salvation wrapped up in Jesus will be the glory of Israel, but it is a light to bring revelation to the Gentiles. Once again, prophecy includes Israel *and* the rest of the world.

■ ■ ■

Paul, the apostle for the Gentiles, sums several prophecies up neatly in Romans, chapter 15. He begins where any good Jew would begin, saying that Jesus came to confirm the promises made to Israel. He doesn't stop there, however, going on to include the Gentiles, saying that Jesus, the Head of the church, came that the Gentiles may glorify God for His mercy.

Then he quotes Deuteronomy, where, early in God's redemption of Israel from Egypt, prophecy says that the Gentiles will rejoice with His people. As the children of Israel are still celebrating their escape from the oppression of Gentiles, God reminds them that the Gentiles are included in His redemptive plan. I wonder if they reflected on how God used Egypt to provide for His people in the famine time of

Joseph and thought that maybe, just maybe, they might be worthy of mercy in the big picture. Big picture thinking is just as important for us as we share in God's plan for mercy for the lost of all nations, tribes and cultures.

Paul then quotes the Psalm which speaks of Gentiles and all people praising and lauding the Lord. Obviously, this was part of Jewish heritage, because it was on God's mind as He shares His overall plan with His people. Throughout His prophetic dealing with Israel, God weaves this thread of the participation of the Gentiles in His plan.

And finally, Paul quotes Isaiah's prophecy about how the root of Jesse will rise to reign over the Gentiles, who will trust in Him. Here again the Gentiles are included in God's redemptive plan, the prophetic basis for the church. Therefore, as Paul writes to the Gentile church in Rome, he talks about how God had always planned for Gentiles to be part of His international church, His people throughout the world.

■ ■ ■

Too often in our focus on Israel or the church we forget that God's plan is a global one. When He created the world, He intended for all people to share in His grace and blessings. When that was disrupted by the fall, plan B went into effect – which was actually plan A, due to the foreknowledge of God – in which Christ was slain from the foundation of the world. Beginning with Adam and Eve, God immediately began to seek and to save that which was lost and continued on that course throughout history, and this included all peoples and nations.

It has always been about sharing the Gospel with the world. The great commission was as valid in the Garden of Eden as it was after the resurrection and as it is today. God has always wanted everyone in the world to share in His wondrous plan for the human race. He expected Adam and Eve to pass that on to their descendants and gave them 900 years to do that. He expected their descendants to pass that on to their descendants so that His wondrous plan would be common knowledge to bless the world.

When the impact of Adam and Eve's ministry faded, Enoch demonstrated what it meant to walk with God, and his subsequent translation made history. At the end of the first epoch of human existence, God called Noah to preach to the world for 120 years. When he had to start over after the flood, Noah passed God's plan on to his family to build their lives on and to pass on to subsequent generations. At each stage in human history, God had His messengers to share His plan with the world.

After Noah's ministry faded, God called out Abraham and his family to take over the job. God's covenant with Abraham specifically included the concept of blessing the whole world. They were to share what they knew about a relationship with God, so that others could enter that relationship, as well.

God's friendship with Abraham was not simply about him and his family. God basically called them out to be missionaries, to share His concern for the world. He has always used earthen vessels to communicate His message with mankind, and He expected Abraham and his family to be actively involved.

God promised to bless Abraham with a big family, numbering more than the sand on the seashore. This would bless, encourage and empower Abraham; but this was not just to bless Abraham, but to multiply the missionaries who would share the Gospel with the nations. God constantly demonstrated His concern for the nations, even when Israel was disobediently not sharing that concern, and He used them even when they were not willing, as we see in the following examples.

■ ■ ■

When Israel was being particularly disobedient, God sent them into captivity in Babylon, the most powerful and extensive empire of the time, an empire ideally suited for the worldwide transmission of the Word of God and His plans for the future. That captivity took Daniel and his friends into Babylon as missionaries, where they did so well that several kings received God's salvation and proclaimed it to the world through official channels, and the "wise men" recorded, studied, and planned for the future in such a way that their descendants showed up in Jerusalem when the promised King was born. What a gracious plan to share the good news with the world, using earthen vessels enabled by the power of God which overcomes serious obstacles to accomplish His purpose in spite of human frailty.

God did similar things with the Jewish captivity in Persia. He used faithful Mordecai and Esther to not only protect His people, but to reach the king with the good news of the plan and the power of the King of kings. And once again, this powerful king used his extensive official channels to pass it on to the world. Thus God used His people and even the Gentiles in His way and His power to reach the lost and to demonstrate His concern for all people.

And then there was Jonah, sent reluctantly to one of Israel's most hated enemies, a people whom God loved enough to offer them salvation. It took some doing, but He finally got Jonah to Nineveh to preach the message of repentance which resulted in the whole city turning to the Lord, much to Jonah's dismay. In spite of human weakness, God used His servant to reach the lost and offer redemption to a nation outside of Israel, thus demonstrating once again His concern for all mankind. Furthermore, Nineveh was at the crossroads of a powerful nation with capabilities of extensive transmission of the message of God's redemptive mercy throughout the region – the logical base for widespread sharing of the Gospel.

Prophecies in Isaiah, Jeremiah, Ezekiel and Daniel concerning Egypt, Ethiopia, Libya, Persia, Greece, the king of the north and the king of the south, etc, showed that the Lord had those nations and peoples on His heart, as well. While He was dealing with Israel in their various stages of obedience and disobedience, God was openly mindful of the nations around them and recorded in these prophets what He was doing and was going to do with the other peoples of the earth, as well, demonstrating again and again that "God so loved the world" included the whole world, not merely the nation of Israel.

■ ■ ■

It was Jewish prophets who, as messengers of God, spoke to His people and, through major communication centers, to all the people of the world. God's plan has, from the beginning, included all peoples and nations; so the Jews should not have been surprised to find that the church was to include the Gentiles, as well. The Old Testament was filled with constant references to God's concern for the world and to His desire to bless the whole world through the Seed of Abraham. The Jews had become so egocentric that they had begun to ignore the global scope of God's plan (sound familiar?).

When Jesus was in the midst of His vast healing ministry, which was one of the prophecies concerning Messiah, He sometimes asked the healed ones not to make Him known. In chapter 12 of his Gospel, Matthew explains that this is a fulfillment of Isaiah 42, which speaks of the Messiah coming for the Gentiles, as well. Obviously, this is a reference to the plan of God which is not exclusive to Israel, but includes the whole world, something the Jews were never excited about.

In His Sermon on the Mount, Jesus references the responsibility Israel still had at that point. He says they are "the salt of the earth, the light of the world, a candle in the dark, and they should let their light shine so that others may be drawn to the Father." He also included the thought that "if the salt had lost its savor, it would be cast out." This is a rather obvious reference to the transition which was to come when the responsibility would be passed to the church during the temporary setting aside of Israel.

After this transition, the church would assume the responsibility of being "the salt of the earth and the light of the world," tasked with bringing the Gospel to the whole world, God's plan from the beginning. This is why prophecy always included references to the Gentiles; so there would be no misunderstanding that the Gospel was, always had been, and always would be for the world, Jew and Gentile alike. When the Old Testament joined the New Testament to form the Bible, it contained this message from start to finish, a constant written reminder that this has always been God's plan.

As we begin our study of the birth of the church, we do well to remember that it follows God's plan which can only be accomplished with His power. Moreover, He has been working on that plan since the beginning of time, and He will see it through to completion. Sometimes we see it as a tiny grain of mustard seed, which doesn't have much chance in a dark and sinful world; but we must remember what Jesus said about how a mustard seed grows. Then we can get involved with confidence and watch God's plan blossom and grow around us and through us. This is the wonderfully encouraging thought of this little book.

Discussion questions:

1. What was God's plan for the church from the beginning? How do we know this?
2. Give several prophecies which illustrate this point.
3. What references to the great commission do we find in the Old Testament? What does this tell us about its relevance throughout history?
4. How do Jewish experiences in Babylon, Persia and Nineveh speak to our church planting efforts?
5. Explain how Jesus tied prophecy into His ministry and directives.
6. Explain how Paul used Old Testament prophecy to encourage a Gentile church.
7. Explain how Peter used Old Testament prophecy to revise his personal outlook and to encourage other Jews within the church.

CHAPTER 3   PREPARATION

"Behold, I send My messenger, and he will prepare the way before Me."
- Malachi 3:1

When God makes a move, He doesn't do things halfway. When God makes a major move like a sustainable plan of redemption for all of mankind, He goes all out to make sure it will not fail, even though failure-prone people will be the key element in the plan. He lays the groundwork throughout the Old Testament, including timetables and indicators to let people know when it will begin. Then He tells them He will send a lead-off messenger to prepare the way when it's about to start.

God always introduces Himself before asking us to belief and usually with corroborating witnesses; because He doesn't want us to miss out, and He wants us to be ready. David saw God help him deal with a lion and a bear before asking him to take on Goliath. Paul heard and saw Christ's ministry and heard Stephen preach, and thus he was ready to respond positively when he met Jesus up close and personal on the road to Damascus. As a young man, I had several experiences with the love and grace of God in my life which prepared me to receive the Savior when someone helped me understand how.

In the same way, as He began to put the next phase of His worldwide plan of redemption into action, God took special pains to prepare the way for Jesus and for the church which would be the continuance of His ministry.

It had been almost 500 years since "the command to restore and build Jerusalem", the beginning of the timeline for Messiah's coming. It had been 400 years since Malachi had announced that a messenger would come. The world was in a Roman rut, and most in Israel had long since quit watching for Messiah. They had things just the way they wanted them, and they languished in the pool of self-satisfaction. They weren't particularly interested in hearing from God and weren't really expecting anything, anyway. This was seen when the wise men came, and the Pharisees told them they should look in Bethlehem but didn't go themselves. Some serious preparation was needed for any serious movement of God, especially for something new and different like the church.

In fact, things were so bad that there had to be preparation for the preparation. An angel had to publicly come to Zacharias to get the rumor going that God was stirring, that something was about to happen. By the time the rumor had run its course "throughout all the hill country of Judea" that an angel had appeared to Zacharias in the temple, John was born to confirm it; and the country began to be expectant again. Six months later there was a kafuffle in Bethlehem about angels singing to shepherds and wise men seeking a king, but the excitement gradually died down, and things returned to normal again. The introduction had been made, however, and when the messenger came, the people would be ready to at least consider his message favorably.

■ ■ ■

When John showed up in the wilderness in his stylish camel hair coat, preaching a baptism of repentance for the remission of sins, the background story of his miraculous birth and angel-announced purpose had been bouncing around the hills for thirty years, and people were interested in what he had to say. Although they didn't come for lunch – they weren't into locusts and wild honey – they lined up to hear him preach and to be baptized. This was the new thing from God which they were waiting for, and they didn't want to miss out.

God was doing something new, something He had been fore-shadowing for millenniums, but He was up to something more than the long hoped for rescue of His people from Roman bondage. John was there to "prepare the way of the Lord", but his ministry went beyond that to prepare the way for the church, the embodiment of God's magnificent plan for the ongoing redemption of His fallen world. John talked about something the chosen people had a hard time understanding when he said "all flesh shall see the salvation of God" – a clear reference to the church. God had long planned to include the Gentiles, and preparation had to be made for that modi-fication in Jewish thought.

■ ■ ■

First, through his preaching and baptizing, John was preparing the people for the Messiah; the One Who would make the whole plan possible. If there was going to be a major change in the Jews' under-standing of God's overall plan, they needed to be ready to accept the change agent. John's assignment was to "go before Him in the spirit and power of Elijah…to make ready a people prepared for the Lord." Therefore, when John's job was done, people would be ready to accept Messiah as the One sent from God to fulfill countless messianic prophecies, including being a light to the Gentiles, an obvious transition in Jewish understanding.

So John, in his Elijah-like garb and utilizing his best Elijah-like preaching voice – the "one crying in the wilderness" that "the kingdom of heaven is at hand" – set out to prepare the way for the Lord. He preached repentance and baptism for the remission of sin; so their hearts would be prepared. When asked if he himself was the One, he constantly denied, saying he was unworthy to even carry the sandals of the mighty One that was coming after Him; so their thought processes would be prepared. He told them that he baptized with water, but that Messiah would baptize with the Holy Spirit and with fire; so their theological perspective would be prepared.

Since it was part of His plan, God was involved in John's ministry. There was power in his preaching which resonated with people, and they flocked to hear him. The Pharisees and even Herod himself came to hear John, the former to hedge their bets and the latter out of curiosity. When Jesus came to be baptized, God was ready to do something special by way of announcement to the crowds gathered around John.

Although John's first reaction was that they had it wrong way around, Jesus assured him that this was the proper way at that particular moment in history. So John obeyed his cousin in fulfillment of his part in God's plan, and God showed him and the attending people the reason for this unlikely turn of events. As Jesus came out of the water after being baptized, the heavens opened, and a dove descended and settled upon Him. There was a voice, "This is My beloved Son, in whom I am well pleased."

■ ■ ■

This was the beginning of John's understanding that Jesus was Messiah. Because he obeyed and baptized Jesus, against his better judgment, that revelation was passed to the crowd, as well, who must have pondered and discussed it for weeks to come. This was one of the ways, perhaps the most startling way, in which John helped prepare a people to accept Messiah. It would be some time before he and the people understood it fully, but the groundwork was laid. A new piece of the puzzle was passed on around the nation which would bear fruit in the months ahead.

This was also the beginning of John's move from general to specific in his identification of Jesus as Messiah. As a result of this transition, people's attention turned to Jesus. This, of course, is what John intended as a fulfillment of his angel-announced mission, even as he was still trying to establish for himself that his cousin was the One. In fact, after he heard that Jesus had raised the widow's son in Nain, John sent disciples to Jesus to clarify this whole concept.

When Jesus delivered the final confirmation, in response to John's question, the crowd understood, because of John's teaching. They understood John's question, "Are You the One?", because he had made it their question, as well. When Jesus answered John's disciples, citing His actions as the fulfillment of Scriptures, the crowd knew what He was saying and what it meant for all of them, because John had pointed the way for that answer to be important.

Ironically, this was the beginning of the end of John's ministry and public importance; but he had already forecast this turn of events, as well. He had told his disciples and the crowd that he must decrease while Messiah increased. John knew his assignment within God's plan and rejoiced in its fulfillment.

■ ■ ■

When Jesus began to do miracles, people made the connection with John's teaching that they should look for someone greater than he was, noting that John, as great a prophet as he was, had done no miracles. Because of what he said, people recognized the Object of John's prophecies when He appeared. Their expectations turned to realization before their very eyes, as what John had said began to come to life. His admonition to look for someone else eased the way for the move from John to Jesus, just what John had intended all along.

His disciples easily made the transition from John to Jesus, because John had taught them what to watch for, and it was apparent that Jesus fit the bill. When they returned to John with the answer that Jesus had given to his question – "Are you the One, or do we seek another?" – I'm sure he used that as his supreme teaching moment to finalize his mission and to prepare them to now begin to follow Messiah. I'm sure he rejoiced to see God's plan come together so perfectly; so he could make the handoff of his followers to the One he was not only telling them about but was also looking forward to himself. When John died, and his disciples went to tell Jesus, it was the most natural thing in the world for them to join up with Jesus, the completion of John's preparation.

■ ■ ■

However, as part of God's plan, John was also preparing the way for the church, even as he prepared the way for Jesus. Dispersed Jews customarily made pilgrimages to Jerusalem for Passover and other special occasions, and, when they did, some must have gone to investigate all the excitement about the preacher in the wilderness. Most likely, some were even baptized by John and took their new understanding and expectations home with them when they returned to their scattered cities of origin. They incorporated this new understanding into their faith and waited from afar for the soon coming of Messiah. The apostles encountered this when they left Jerusalem after the resurrection to take the gospel to the world.

One city where they came across this was Ephesus. Paul found a group of Jews who had been baptized "into John's baptism". When Paul took it from there and explained that Christ had come, the Messiah John spoke about; these Jews believed and were baptized in Jesus' name. In this way, John's ministry prepared the way for the church in Ephesus and, I'm sure, in other cities, as well.

Meanwhile, in Corinth, a fervent young preacher from Ephesus had come to preach. Apollos was "an eloquent man and mighty in the Scriptures". He had come to Ephesus from Alexandria and had been taught the baptism of John. When he went on to Corinth to pass it along, he met Aquilla and Priscilla, Paul's tent making friends. They took him the next step, telling him, too, that Christ had come, the Messiah John told them to watch for, and Apollos became a great preacher of the gospel and a great encourager of the early church. Once again, John's ministry prepared the way.

As God commenced His plan for the church which would stretch 2000 years into the future, He used John to prepare the way for Jesus' ministry in Israel and for the birth of the church in scattered cities throughout the region. The Lord is a good planner and a careful builder. His plans come to fruition, because He knows how to make them work and provides the wisdom and power to do so.

Discussion questions:

1. Why did God send John, the Baptist?
2. What two means did John use to announce that Jesus was the Messiah?
3. How did John prepare his disciples and the people for the transition from following him to following Jesus?
4. How do we know that God also used John to prepare the way for the church?

CHAPTER 4   JESUS HIMSELF

"...Jesus Himself drew near and went with them."
- Luke 24:15

We have already established that Jesus came to lay the groundwork for the church, even as He was paying the price for its existence and its continuity. Now we look at some details of that groundwork, details and concepts too often overlooked with the assumption that the church did not begin until Pentecost, some forty days after His death. This assumption is technically correct, but, obviously, Jesus, Who knew the plan since before the world began, would prepare those who would bear the responsibility.

And herein lies the key. In our modern church planting theories the emphasis is on method, whereas His emphasis was on people – the earthen vessels He would empower to take the Gospel to the world. He poured His life into a few branches who would produce much fruit – self-sustaining and self-propagating fruit – as they drew on the resources of the Vine.

This is His groundwork in a nutshell, a concept so simple as to not be taken seriously in our present, complicated, "there must be something more to it" world. And yet that simple approach has been unfailing, even with all the fallible people involved, because it has been, and always will be, based upon His plan and His power, rather than on human strategies and human energy. In fact, it seems to work best under the worst of human conditions, which is why it continues undiminished today, some 2000 years later. It's why it worked with Bruce Olsen, who wandered into the jungle with nothing more than His plan and His power.

■ ■ ■

Jesus began with the twelve, twelve ordinary, unassuming sinners who needed His mercy to even be considered for ministry, much less to be the building blocks of the church, which would be the living, self-replicating extension of Himself. It was as if He chose the most unlikely people to demonstrate that He could use anyone, that His power could compensate for any human weakness and accomplish something amazing. Paul summed it up as choosing the foolish, the weak, the base, the despised, and the things which are not; because the foolishness of God is wiser than men, and the weakness of God is stronger than men.

Watching those twelve in action through the Gospel accounts would cause one to despair of the present, to say nothing of the future. Peter was constantly putting his foot in it. James and John were always angling for advantage, even bringing their mother along to lobby for them. Judas "borrowed" money from the till. They all had a hard time with faith, even as Jesus did miracle after miracle before their very eyes. They argued with each other. They argued with Him about going to Jerusalem. These guys will be the basis of the church!? What kind of idea was that? And how could it possibly work?

Jesus took them everywhere He went, so they saw everything He did, heard everything He said, experienced everything He experienced, and watched how the world reacted to Him. They saw Him heal the sick, calm the storm, raise the dead and preach the Gospel. They watched Him answer antagonistic questions and handle Himself with quiet respect for people of all persuasions and agendas, even as He retained His integrity and His faithfulness to the Father Who sent Him. This was training by osmosis.

Then there were the hands-on experiences. They helped to miraculously feed the two crowds which numbered in the thousands. Peter walked on the water...for a while. Peter, James and John experienced the transfiguration. They all went out on the first mission trip with an extensive mission brief from Jesus, and they watched it all work for themselves as they preached and healed in His power.

Then there were the wrap up sessions recorded in the last few chapters of John. There was a lesson on servant leadership in chapter 13. There were promises of His abiding care, provisions and presence in chapter14. He summed up His relationship with them and how that would carry into their ministry to the world in chapter 15. He explained how the Holy Spirit would empower them for that ministry in chapter 16. And He prayed for them (and the future church) in chapter 17.

And we must not overlook the après resurrection sessions where Jesus got the eleven back on track, solidified in their faith and pointed in the right direction. He let Peter know he was forgiven for his denial and gave him his leadership assignment in the church. He answered Thomas' questions and called him to a steady faith (as a result, Thomas is still honored in India for his church planting ministry there). He answered theological questions on the road to Emmaus and "opened their understanding" in the upper room. He met with them all in Galilee and gave them the great commission – the authority and the power to be the church to the end of the age. For forty days He lived the promise and power of the resurrection for them.

This is just a brief summary of Christ's personal ministry with the twelve who would carry on His work – to be the church and the beginning of the self-propagating church which continues today. He poured His life into them. He loved them, taught them, corrected their mistakes and answered their questions, while vividly demonstrating what He was saying, so they could understand because they could see it. They would be the earthen vessels empowered by the Holy Spirit to be the basis of the church; so He concentrated on them as the key to the future.

They would also be the archives of the Jesus-on-earth experience. This makes me think of the new presidential library which just opened – the George W. Bush presidential library – which was designed not only to preserve Bush's papers, but also to be an interactive experience with the Bush presidency. This same concept sums up the job of the apostles – they preserved Jesus' "papers", as the Holy Spirit brought them to memory; but they also provided an interactive experience with Jesus' residency here on earth. Matthew and John wrote down their memories, aided by the Holy Spirit; but all the apostles were available for interaction with the early church, passing on their personal connection with Jesus to those who would pass it on from there.

■ ■ ■

But there's more to His preparation for the church. We often overlook the seventy and the others He trained in similar ways. There must have been some kind of extended training program, because

He sent the seventy out on a mission trip, too, again with a mission brief before they left. They knew Jesus well enough to follow those instructions faithfully, to watch them work, and to come back with joy that even the demons were subject to them in His name. In other words, they, too, had experienced the grace and power of Jesus which prepared them to be vital members of the church when He was gone. The replacement apostle chosen to fill Judas' spot may have been from this group.

But that's still not all. There were approximately forty more (to round out the 120 gathered at Pentecost), mainly support personnel, who followed Jesus closely, as well. They heard and saw everything with eager hearts, some probably taught by John and all ready to follow Jesus when they had personal contact with Him. Some had experienced His personal healing ministry. Some of them were first at the tomb after the resurrection. They were all at the prayer meetings leading up to Pentecost. And they were all part of the birth of the church.

So Jesus was preparing a fairly large group to be the basis for the church. He personally trained and taught and cared for them. They had experienced His ministry firsthand. They had heard His teachings and watched His love in action as they helped care for His earthly needs. They had been at Calvary, felt the earthquake and watched the sun go dark. They had shared in the joy of the resurrection. So when it came time for Him to go home and for the church to be launched, they were ready to help carry on His work, since they all had known Him personally and loved to share that relationship with others.

This was the core of how Jesus prepared the way for the church within His earthly ministry. These were the core people He poured Himself into, so they could "pass it on." These were the people prepared by Jesus Himself to know and understand what was on His heart, so they could be "springs of living water", overflowing in their world, "springing up unto eternal life" for all they met. They were ready, not to "do church", but to be the church which would take His heart to the world for 2000 years to come.

■ ■ ■

However, there were still more that Jesus prepared to share in the birth of the church – the Pharisees, for example, perhaps for their training in the scriptures which would provide theological underpinnings for the embryonic church as it was getting its feet under it. We are most familiar with Jesus' theological session with the Pharisee, Nicodemus, who went on to speak up for Jesus at strategic times, and even helped Joseph of Arimathea bury the body of Jesus after the crucifixion. And there was the rich young ruler Jesus' heart went out to when he came with questions and grieved for when he turned away. But Jesus was extraordinarily patient with all the Pharisees, even as they plotted against Him and attacked Him publicly.

He answered their questions so well that they finally decided not to ask Him any more questions, because He always seemed to come out ahead. But in those shrewd and perceptive answers, the Pharisees, who were used to lively theological debates among themselves, received basic training which would prepare them to be part of the early church when they were ready. And some, along with a "great many of the priests" (more leader types who had theological training), did believe after the resurrection, the resurrection which was a fulfillment of the sign they requested. Jesus said He would only give them the sign of Jonah, and I'm sure they understood the significance of that when Jesus returned after three days in the grave.

And then there was Paul, a Pharisee and proud of it. He watched and listened from the fringes as Jesus taught and did miracles and died and rose again. He listened as Stephen preached a beautiful summary of the Gospel in relation to Paul's beloved nation of Israel. He watched as Stephen suddenly saw Jesus standing at the right hand of God and watched him die with that glory on his face. Then Paul came face to face with Jesus Himself on the road to Damascus and began the process of yielding completely to the risen Savior. But that was just the beginning of Jesus' personal ministry to Paul in preparation for his role in the church.

In the first chapter of Galatians, Paul explains his first three years as a believer and what he received "through the revelation of Jesus Christ." He goes on to tell how God "revealed His Son in me, that I might preach Him among the Gentiles". Apparently he spent about three years in fellowship with Jesus this way before going to Jerusalem to see Peter. In other words, Jesus Himself was preparing Paul, the Pharisee, to provide theological groundwork for the emerging church, groundwork we rely on even today.

■ ■ ■

What Jesus did not do: An interesting side note at this point is what Jesus did ***not*** do as He laid the foundation for the church and did the training which would sustain it for two thousand years. Seeing what He did not do is just as important as watching what He did do, if we are to understand His plan and His power for His body, the church.

He never invited people to join a church, even though a church was what He was planning, and, in our way of thinking, this would be the ideal opportunity to do so – to strike while the iron was hot, to get their names on the dotted line while the interest was immediate and intense. In fact, when the woman at the well gave Him the perfect opening – "you worship in Jerusalem, but we worship here" – He didn't take advantage of that opportunity to invite her to join Him at the "correct" place. He told her instead that God is Spirit and must be worshipped in spirit and in truth, no matter the location.

He didn't invite her to His church. He invited her to come home to His Father, as Paul summed up so well – "God was in Christ, reconciling the world unto Himself." Paul goes on to say that we, too, are called to that ministry, not inviting people to church, but, as His ambassadors, helping them "be reconciled to God." That concept will give new life to our ministry and will keep witnessing and church planting in the proper perspective.

The disciples were in the "you should come to our church" mode and would have completely missed what was happening around the well in Samaria, except that Jesus told them to "lift up their eyes, for the fields are white, ready for harvest." Even then, they must have looked around and thought, "Where? There's no one here but a bunch of accursed Samaritans."

They may have begun to understand when they followed Jesus into town for a two day visit which resulted in many believers; but I'm sure it was difficult for them even then. How like us they were, thinking about the exclusivity of their "church" and how people simply needed to come to their "church" in order to be of any value. This was just one of the first lessons Jesus gave them (and us) about how the gospel was for everyone, and we are to invite people to share the joy of reconciliation to the Father, Who must be worshipped in spirit and in truth, rather than at a particular place.

■ ■ ■

Another thing which Jesus did **not** do was to begin to provide organizational structure for His new movement. In our way of thinking, the coming church would never survive long without governing guidelines and at least a proper set of bylaws and church officers. And yet, as we have seen, Jesus, who had a comprehensive plan which would carry the church far into the future, gave it no structure, bylaws or officers. In fact, when James and John and their lobbyist mother announced their candidacy for vice-president, Jesus told them (and the rest of His disciples, including us) that the only candidacy was for service and sacrifice.

As Paul pointed out later, Jesus was not concerned about organization and bylaws because the church was His body. He was its head, and everyone else reported directly to Him, although there were different functions within the body. Although humans like organizational flow charts, and Paul developed several slots for people to fit into for leadership needs, Jesus always saw Himself as directly responsible, as we will see in a moment. We would do well to keep this in mind as we labor within the contemporary church; so we don't get caught up in human planning and structure and lose sight of, and lose the power of, Jesus' original intent.

■ ■ ■

However, there was more to Jesus' planning and preparation for the early church. We have seen the extensive groundwork He laid for the church, preparing people to be the church, and we have seen what He did not do. We have seen His follow-up work with the disciples and with Paul after His resurrection which started the church off on the right track. Now we look at His follow-up with individual churches through those early years which insured that they stayed on the right track.

With several of the apostles martyred and other church leaders scattered by persecution, Jesus still insured that He would have a spokesman to speak to the churches for Him when He had John exiled to Patmos and protected there. Before revealing His plan for the last days, Jesus first had a few notes for the early church, of which He was responsible, as the Head. These He also entrusted to John, knowing they would be taken seriously and passed on to the churches He named specifically. Those instructions are valuable for the modern church, and it is appropriate to use them so; but they were written for specific early churches with specific problems in specific cities.

Ephesus did have a problem with being absorbed in works and striving for purity and having "left their first love." Jesus personally commended them, but then called them back to Himself. How He longed for them (and us) to simply stay close to Him and specifically, personally told them so. We can only imagine the impact this message had for the Ephesians, being reminded of His personal attention to them and their efforts and hearing His personal love for them again. I feel certain they must have repented anxiously and then renewed their love for their Savior and Friend. They must have treasured this personal message from Jesus, and it probably carried that church many years down the road.

The church in Smyrna must have also been greatly encouraged by a personal word from the Lord Himself. He told them He knew their situation, their testings and trials and encouraged them to be faithful and unafraid. With that special word from Jesus, Whom they knew had faced great trials, how they must have been uplifted and strengthened to face hard things of their own, secure in His love and in His reminder of eternal life. This must have been just the powerful word, at just the right time, which they needed to face dark times without fear. What a difference it must have made for that church, and it must have carried them many years down the road, as well.

To the church in Pergamos, Jesus had words of admonition, as well as words of encouragement. What an amazing demonstration of the fact that no secrets are hidden from Him and that He cares enough to do something about them, as He also reminds them that He only has the best in mind for them. I like to think that those He admonished heard His love and His authority and did repent and that the church prospered for many years afterward, representing Him well in that city.

There were problems in Thyatira, and Jesus addressed them specifically while encouraging those not involved. He reminded them that He searches the minds and the hearts and that He will do something about what He finds. He also reminded those who were trying to do the right thing that He understood their burden, encouraging them to be faithful. Once again, consider the effect a personal, specific word from Jesus would have had. He was going to deal with the problem so they could see His personal involvement with their church. When they saw the problem people dealt with according to His specifically stated plan, the others must have been greatly encouraged to persevere in their city.

Sardis is a different story, of which Jesus knows the details and addresses them personally. He encourages those who seek to be faithful, which must have blessed them, as they probably thought no one noticed. And he speaks specifically and in detail to those who are simply putting on a good show, without substance, calling them to repentance. We can only imagine the effect His admonition had on this church; but we can clearly see His concern and care for His body and His willingness to be actively involved in doing something about it.

Philadelphia was a fragile, but faithful church in a tough situation. How they must have appreciated a word of power and encouragement from the King of kings and Lord of lords, Who said He has opened a door for them which no one can shut. He tells them He will be active on their behalf and will be their defense in their time of trial. He tells them they are His treasures, and He will care for them. How that must have uplifted them and strengthened them to persevere. What a beautiful picture of Jesus' active involvement with and personal care for His new churches.

To Laodicea, He says, "As many as I love, I rebuke and chasten." They were a passionless church which had gotten off track in pursuit of worldly gain. Instead of condemnation, which they so richly deserve, He loves them, offering healing and genuine riches in terms which are highly localized, specific to their city. This is the Good Shepherd at His best, personally caring for His flock where they are. The Laodiceans would have heard the love coming through and probably would have at least tried to respond in positive ways to such specific instructions.

And Jesus concludes His messages to His churches by reminding them that He is always available to help. "Behold, I stand at the door and knock...if you open the door, I will come in..." These are His churches, redeemed by His blood, planted at His command and cared for by His incredible love and concern and power. Paul sums it up well when he tells us this about God's plan, "He who did not spare His own Son, but delivered Him up for us all, how shall He not with Him also freely give us all things?" Jesus already has so much invested in the newborn church that He is ready to follow up in any way necessary to insure its success.

That personal ministry continues today. When Bruce Olson's father rejected him for his growing faith in the living Savior, Jesus

Himself ministered to Bruce to encourage him, lift him and stand with him. The story of His personal ministry to and through him as he went to share the Gospel with the jungle tribe in South America is a modern example of Jesus' direct involvement with His people and His church. It's also a reminder of our need to work with Jesus as we seek to do our part in His church.

■ ■ ■

The church was His body, so Jesus did extensive preparations to insure the fulfillment of His plan. He spent three and a half years with the people who would be the building blocks of the church, personally training and empowering the twelve, the seventy and the rest of the 120, including critical time after the resurrection. He was patient with the Pharisees, who would go on to be the theological foundation of the church. He did personal, specific follow up with the churches that sprang up throughout the region, insuring steady, faithful growth and perseverance even in difficult locations. Jesus was and always will be personally involved with the church. Understanding that will give the same encouragement and empowering to us as it did to them.

Discussion questions:

1. What was Jesus' main focus as He laid the groundwork for the church? What can we learn from that?
2. What were the four different groups Jesus worked with to prepare them for taking their place in the church?
3. Summarize the different means Jesus used to train the apostles.

4. How did Jesus train the Pharisees for their place in the church? When did they take that place?
5. How did Jesus prepare Paul for his role in the church?
6. What did Jesus *not* do in His training of the early believers?
7. Who was Jesus' spokesman to the early church? How did he demonstrate Jesus' personal involvement with individual churches?
8. Summarize how Jesus laid the foundation for the church which would carry it for 2000 years.

CHAPTER 5   POWER

*Jesus said, "All power is given to Me in heaven and in Earth...
go therefore..." - Matthew 28:18-19*

If Jesus was calling earthen vessels to carry out His plan, which was to be the church, vital and self-sustaining for 2000 years, He was going to have to provide the power for that plan, or else it would surely fail, brought down by human weakness. If He was going to count on the church surviving beyond the first generation of those who had personal experience with Him, He was going to have to provide a source of power which would never diminish, constant and consistent to lift people above themselves and above their circumstances, personally connected with Him. The One who spoke the world into being and holds it all together by His awesome power was going to have to provide a way for that power to be available to those who would be the branches, His body, the church.

That power would have to be available to every goodhearted volunteer, no matter their age, ability or experience, if they were to be effective. That power would have to be available wherever it was needed, no matter the location, situation, language or culture, if it was to carry the church to the uttermost parts of the earth. That power would have to be available whenever it was needed, readily available so that no opportunity would be lost, no crisis would be overwhelming and none of His little ones would be defenseless. An effective plan of the incredible scope Jesus had in mind would have to include this power, and He had exactly that in mind from the very beginning, a brilliant concept with amazing possibilities.

The disciples, first the twelve and then the seventy, had already experienced that power on their initial mission trips. They saw people healed, demons cast out and hearts opened to Messiah's coming, and they knew it was because of the power now available to them through Jesus' name. This was their first taste of the power they would need to carry out their responsibilities as the church, experienced before they had any concept of the church or any responsibilities in it.

Jesus explained this further in the wrap-up sessions before His death, as He told them about the ministry of the Holy Spirit, whom He would send to them. He explained that the Holy Spirit would be their comforter, teacher and enabler, even as He fulfilled His role of convicter of souls. Jesus went on to tell them that the Holy Spirit would work alongside them to testify of Him. In other words, in the person of the Holy Spirit, the power would be available for them to fulfill the massive assignment He was giving them as He went home after finishing His part of the plan.

As He was saying good-bye and ascending into the clouds, He told them to wait in Jerusalem until they received the fullness of that power before attempting to take the Gospel to the world. Thus, as the 120 gathered in the upper room to pray, it was not about praying for power. Jesus had already promised that. They simply needed to wait, and, as they waited, it seemed obvious to pray. And since the naming of a replacement apostle came out of that prayer time, one could assume that they were praying for themselves as they faced the great commission together. It was obvious they were going to need supernatural power, so they waited for that power, as Jesus told them to.

They could not have expected what happened at Pentecost, but, although Peter thought it was some end days phenomenon, I am sure that it was a perfectly understandable object lesson in the power that was now available. Jesus had said to wait for the power, and now here it was in full force and obvious in purpose. Although it must have been a glorious experience, it was clearly not intended to simply be a thrill or to be personally edifying. That power was intended for the task Jesus had given them. They watched in amazement as it enabled them to share the Gospel in the heart language of thousands of visitors the Lord had brought to Jerusalem at just the right moment to receive the seed which would grow into new branches of the Vine all over the region, churches sprouting throughout the Mediterranean world. And as time went on, the apostles continued in that power, doing many signs and wonders to help establish the emerging church.

What an incredible beginning for the newborn church. As the Holy Spirit powered the message through earthen vessels to thousands of hearers, many received it gladly. Three thousand new believers entered the ranks on opening day, the first fruit on the Vine. As they joined the fellowship of teaching, prayer, breaking of bread and worship, each of them began to draw on that power, as well, had a positive impact on the people around them, and "the Lord added to the church daily those who were being saved."

When Peter and John went, in that power, up to the temple, healed a lame man and preached to the ensuing crowd, 5000 more believed. Now there were approximately 10,000 who gathered to hear Peter and John report how the chief priests and elders had threatened them. 10,000 who asked God for boldness and power to share the Gospel. 10,000 who gave themselves to the Lord and to each other to be the body of Christ and to minister to the world around them. 10,000 who now needed the power to be the church in a fallen world, hostile territory which would just as soon see the church fade into insignificance.

■ ■ ■

Ironically, one of the first things that utilized the power in those early days was a disciplinary problem, which highlights the Lord's concern for the integrity of His body and His willingness to do something about it. Ananias and Sapphira were selfish and thought no one would notice if they had the best of both worlds. They severely underestimated the power involved in the church and the seriousness of sin within that context, and they paid with their lives. It's His church, and we would do well to remember that before we try to manipulate it to fit our personal agendas. Apparently, the surrounding world appreciated the integrity demonstrated, because "multitudes" of believers were added to the Lord as a result of that incident.

The power would also get people into trouble, when it brought them up against a world set in its ways. The power enabled much healing in Jerusalem, and somehow the high priests felt threatened and put the apostles in prison, thinking that would slow things down. The Lord had other things in mind, sent an angel to release them and gave them an opportunity to speak for Him before the council. It cost them a beating, but they rejoiced that they were counted worthy to suffer for Jesus' name and continued to preach and teach Christ daily wherever they could. The power was available, and His grace was sufficient for His work.

With believers numbering over 10,000, the apostles needed help with ministry and would soon discover whether or not the power was transferable. They simply asked the church to nominate seven men of good report, full of the Holy Ghost and wisdom. Apparently this was not an unreasonable request, as the church was "pleased", fully understanding the standards and the need for them, and came up with seven outstanding candidates, seven seemingly random people with no mention of experience, education or coming up through the ranks.

There seemed to be no further discussion or voting. The apostles merely acknowledged their choices, prayed for them, laid hands on them and turned them loose with full authority, confident in the Holy Spirit's power and leading for their ensuing ministry. Although we only have details about Stephen and Phillip, the first leadership team obviously lived up to expectations, as "the number of disciples multiplied greatly in Jerusalem", including a "great company of priests." Obviously, the power was transferable, a good sign for the church in the next 2000 years.

■ ■ ■

Without further fanfare, training or probation period, Stephen began to minister in that power. He did "great wonders and miracles among the people", and apparently the apostles felt totally unthreatened. They acted as though this was completely expected, absolutely necessary, in fact, if the church was to flourish, which was the point. As the years went on, I'm sure they began to count on this multiplying effect of the power, as they watched Jesus continue to build His church. They may even have begun to feel a little like John the Baptist as they got older – "we must decrease, but they must increase" – as they finished their courses and watched the next generation assume the responsibility for the future of the church. Knowing that the power was fully transferable must have been very reassuring at that point.

That same power made Stephen a compelling preacher and teacher, and those who opposed him "were not able to resist the wisdom and the spirit by which he spoke." The next major sermon in the church was delivered, not by Peter or John, but by Stephen. As he poured out his heart before a hostile crowd, they saw glory on his face, "as if it was the face of an angel", and they listened to a lengthy discourse on the history of rebellion, only interrupting him when he became severely personal about their rejection of Christ.

Even then, they could not refute the power or the point of what he was saying, and they had to resort to violence. When, in the face of their opposition, he saw Jesus standing at the right hand of God and declared as much, their only recourse was to kill him. The power which had transferred to him when he assumed his leadership role not only enabled him to endure stoning, but to glorify God in the midst of it. That was the power which would sustain the church for 2000 years without losing its force.

Phillip got carried away, as perhaps we all should, not because he was "ordained", but because he understood the purpose of the power. When Saul's harassment scattered the church according to God's plan outlined in Acts 1:8, Phillip went to Samaria, preaching Christ and doing miracles, which caused great joy in that city. When many were baptized and then received the Holy Spirit through Peter and John's follow-up ministry, the power came to that city to further extend the church. The power transfer to the leadership team was paying off in a big way, but Phillip was not done.

When he shared the gospel in the desert with a eunuch who had great authority in a queen's retinue, he planted seeds for a church in Ethiopia. As he preached on through neighboring cities, Phillip planted seeds for the church throughout the rest of that region. The purpose of the power was to fulfill the great commission, and it had that effect when it was transferred to Phillip and, I'm sure, to the others, as well.

Thus the power was transferred down through the years, not through human device or strategy, but by the Holy Spirit as He willed. This power, greater than the most powerful nuclear generator, has powered and sustained the church for 2000 years, so that the life force of Jesus Himself has been transferred over and over again without diminishing and without change, a truly amazing thing. The power that gave birth to the church on Pentecost is available today for the same purpose, as Bruce Olson experienced in the jungles of South America, and as any and every good hearted volunteer has experienced worldwide.

Then the power was passed on to me, not to have some powerful ministry, but to be able to pass on the life force of Jesus to others. It has been my privilege and blessing to share Jesus with innumerable people from all age groups and all walks of life and to watch them make a life-changing connection with the living Savior and, in turn, watch that power enable them to pass it on to others with the same effect. This was not the result of my ordination or of some secret prayer on my part, but as a part of God's plan for the church, the living extension of the Vine through the power of the Holy Spirit. Jesus planned it, prepared for it, paid for it and powered it, and the effectiveness of that plan continues undiminished today.

As we consider the principles of His design for the power for His plan, how it worked at the beginning and how it has worked steadily throughout church history, we do well to take those principles into consideration as we pray and plan and work in the church today. His plan and His power always far exceed any human strategy, energy or effort we can discover or exert, and we do well to connect with that plan and power before we try any we might design. He has already designed the all-sufficient power for this amazing plan of His and only the proper use of that power within the guidelines of that plan will yield worthwhile results.

Discussion questions:

1. Why did the church need supernatural power? What were the elements of that power needed for the church to be successful?
2. What was the disciples' first experience with that power?
3. What did they experience with that power at Pentecost? What significance did that have for the birth of the church?
4. How did the disciples find out that the power was transferable? What significance did that have for the birth and sustainability of the church?
5. How do we know that the power is still available undiminished today? And for what purpose?

CHAPTER 6   FIRST WAVE

*"You shall receive power...and you shall be witnesses for Me...
in Jerusalem, in all Judea, and in Samaria..." - Acts 1:8*

At His ascension, Jesus gave the church the basic outline for the great commission—Jerusalem, Judea, Samaria, then the rest of the world—but there wasn't much church there. Those who were there must have wondered how 120 people were supposed to reach the whole world, no matter how empowered or enthusiastic they might be. So they waited for the power, little realizing that they were waiting for the rest of the church, soon to join them to carry out His instructions.

It must have been a greatly encouraging surprise for the 120 to find that Jesus was not expecting them to reach the world themselves, but to provide basic training for the 10,000 He was sending to join them in the days immediately following Pentecost. Instead of huddling in the upper room, praying over their impossible assignment and trying to find a replacement apostle to help them, they found themselves powerfully filled with the Spirit and surrounded by thousands of new believers who were anxious to be part of the plan to reach the world. Any anxiety the 120 might have felt over the difficult responsibility given them by Jesus was washed away by the joy and overwhelming exuberance of 10,000 eager to learn and eager to help them.

Now it became obvious how they were supposed to reach the world, a world which Jesus had brought to them. Jews from all over the Roman Empire, from Asia to North Africa, who had come to Jerusalem for the holy days, were hungrily trying to understand the awesome resurrection message which they would take home with them. At some point it would have dawned on the 120 that they had the opportunity to multiply their efforts by 10,000 to be scattered throughout the known world. They were more occupied trying to train these new converts than to worry about what they themselves would do next. They were swept up in what clearly had been Jesus' plan all along as He told them, "The Spirit shall testify of Me, and you also shall bear witness, because you have been with Me from the beginning." They were simply the human messengers who would pass on what they had received from Jesus to those 10,000 human messengers who would carry the message to the world.

■ ■ ■

Those early glory days of the church must have been wonderful. Thousands of new believers mingling with the core group of disciples riding the euphoria of Pentecost in Jerusalem. It was all so new and amazing, and they couldn't get enough of it. Worshipping every day in the temple and sharing communion from house to house "with gladness and singleness of heart", they were constantly "praising God and having favor with all the people." They didn't want to go home.

They wanted to hear everything about Jesus. They had heard summaries in the first sermons from Peter and Stephen, but now they wanted to hear the rest of the story, a story that only those who had been with Jesus from the beginning could tell. With eager new believers gathered around, the "residential library" kicked into high gear. The apostles shared all the things Jesus had taught them, all the miraculous things He had done and all the things that He was, which only personal experience could relate. They taught them how to pray, and they prayed together. Most of all they shared fellowship with the risen Savior together, so these new believers could build the personal relationship with Jesus which would carry them through the difficult circumstances they would face when they returned to their corner of the world. With such a mountaintop experience, who could blame them for reluctance to go home?

When they pooled their resources, they even had enough money to continue in this dreamlike lifestyle for a while. They sold houses and land in order to linger there as long as possible, learning and growing, rejoicing and getting stronger personally and as a group. But those halcyon days were simply the incubator, never intended to be a permanent condition. We would do well to remember that before we try to build a church to be like that newborn church in Jerusalem, no matter how wonderful it sounded. Sooner or later that fledgling church was going to have to leave the nest and fly, as Jesus had intended and had, in fact, commanded. The world was waiting, and those amazing early experiences were merely the beginning, not the end.

Like a mother eagle, God knew that baby eagles were not meant to spend their lives safely in a mountaintop nest, no matter how glorious the situation. Like a mother eagle, God provided the impetus when it was time for the church to spread its wings and begin to fulfill the great commission, beginning with their surrounding cities, as Jesus had outlined for them at His ascension. Like a mother eagle, God made it uncomfortable for a church which was ready to fly, a church which had grown comfortable basking in the glory of the resurrection, the flames of Spirit fire and the warmth and popularity of the burgeoning fellowship of kindred spirits. We would do well to remember that when we get overly comfortable in our contemporary church experience.

After the stoning of Stephen, "there was a great persecution against the church in Jerusalem." This persecution could have easily been classified as an attack from the devil, as we are so wont to do these days. However, when the results fit so perfectly with the outline for the church given by Jesus at His ascension, it becomes obvious that this was mother eagle action on God's part as the beginning of the next phase in His plan. The incubator bubble burst, the warming lamp was turned off, and the energetic new church, fresh out of basic training, was "scattered throughout the regions of Judea and Samaria", leaving the apostles at the base camp in Jerusalem. The first wave of the great commission had begun.

It may be instructive to note at this point that we will see Paul use this same process in his ministry. He would have an intense, but fairly brief, period of basic training in a city before entrusting the new church to local believers, trusting the plan and the power for good results as he moved on to a new place to start over. God has a tendency to stick with what works. Now back to the first wave.

. . .

Although we only have record of Phillip's ministry, we can easily assume that this was merely one example of the first wave, as all those who were scattered through the surrounding region "went everywhere preaching the word." That same energy and enthusiasm they shared in Jerusalem simply spilled out into the adjoining cities and towns, fulfilling Jesus' prophecy that the water He would give would "be in them a well of water springing up unto everlasting life." The power which Jesus had provided for His earthen vessels would have an effect similar to what Phillip experienced, and this first wave would have had similar experiences in all the neighboring areas.

The first century grapevine would have spread rumors throughout the region that something extraordinary was happening in Jerusalem, and the people who hadn't made the pilgrimage would have been eager for word from witnesses. When witnesses began to filter throughout the outlying areas of Judea and Samaria they would have attracted eager crowds anxious for first-hand information. At that point, the plan and the power would have gone into action again. The Spirit would have testified of Jesus, and the newly trained believers from Jerusalem would have shared their experiences, helping interested listeners find for themselves a personal relationship with the Savior.

When you spread 10,000 eager missionaries across a relatively small area, there would be good coverage, as well as interwoven support, and the church planting would have been extensive. Every city, town and hamlet would have heard the message as pilgrims went home and other scattered believers shared their joy. Later accounts from the book of Acts confirm that churches sprang up in Damascus, Antioch, Lydda, Joppa, Phoenicia and Cyprus, although these must have merely been examples of the cities and towns reached by this first wave.

It's not a big stretch of the imagination to assume that, as news similar to Phillip's began to come in from other towns, one of the apostles would have been sent for follow up ministry. He would have offered basic training, fellowship, prayer and power to ensure that the seedling church got off to a good start in that location. In this way

Jesus' outline for the church would have been carried out. There were churches "throughout all Judea and Galilee and Samaria" by the time Paul was converted. When his rampage ended that way, the record shows that those churches "had rest...were edified; and walking in the fear of the Lord and in the comfort of the Holy Spirit, were multiplied." These were first wave churches, alive and growing, the result of the ministry of the first 10,000 out of basic training.

■ ■ ■

The Book of Acts gives us a brief tour of some of these churches. Peter was doing follow up ministry "through all parts of the country" when he went to visit the church in Lydda, a church which was already there on the border of Judea and Samaria as a result of this first wave. While he was there, he healed a man, and many in that town and the adjoining town of Saron saw it and turned to the Lord. So the work of the early church scattered from Jerusalem was strengthened and increased by follow up from Peter, and then he moved on.

He moved on because the first wave church in Joppa, the next town over, heard that Peter was in Lydda and asked him to come heal Dorcas, one of the church members there. Perhaps Peter was beginning to see a pattern evolving concerning early church planting and growth, because he left the newly strengthened church in Lydda and went to Joppa. He healed Dorcas; "many believed in the Lord"; and the church flourished during the "many days" he spent there, lodging with Simon the tanner, a local church member.

The plan was going into effect, as summed up later by Paul. Some of the scattered church from Jerusalem planted, Peter watered, and God gave the increase. How many times this must have happened throughout the region as the fledgling church spread its wings, forced out of the nest to share the Gospel with the surrounding area, and backed up by the apostles out of Home Base Jerusalem.

■ ■ ■

God Himself initiated the next move, paving the way for phase two – ministry to the Gentiles. He sends word to Cornelius, a centurion sent to Caesarea by the Romans, thus being there to be the first step in fulfilling God's plan for the Gentiles. It's no coincidence that God uses a person of such status to initiate this phase, because when he is instructed to send for Peter, Cornelius has the authority and the decisiveness to do so that very day.

Meanwhile, back at Simon the tanner's, God is having a briefing with Peter to lay out the upcoming mission. Peter, a good Jew, needed an attitude adjustment before he would step foot in the house of a Gentile, and an occupying Roman centurion, at that, despite Old Testament prophecies about taking the Gospel to the Gentiles and despite Jesus' example of reaching out to Gentiles. As God was finishing His "clean and unclean" briefing with Peter, the messengers from Cornelius arrived at the door to find Peter now willing to go, something they never doubted.

When Peter and company arrived at Cornelius' house, he found the soon-to-be Gentile church in Caesarea gathered there, waiting to hear the message God sent him to bring. After he explained how unusual this was for a Jew to be there, Peter went on to tell what he'd learned. Beginning with his new understanding that the Gospel is available, and desirable, for all nations, he went on to preach Jesus, His death and resurrection, and His invitation for all to receive forgiveness of sins. As he finished his message, God got involved again, which was to be expected, because it was His plan.

The Holy Spirit fell, as at Pentecost; and these new Gentile believers began to speak in tongues to magnify the Lord. Obviously, the Lord was including Gentiles in the church and empowering them, and Peter commanded them to be baptized to signify just that. Then he stayed in Caesarea to see this new little church established, since this was part of the apostles' responsibility in this first wave.

Now there must be a communication of this new development. The early church needed a respected voice to interpret this astonishing phenomenon within the framework of developing theology and strategy. This is why God had Peter on the scene to witness this transition, knowing personally that it was from God Himself. God had planned this so Peter could testify of this new concept's actuality and importance to headquarters in Jerusalem. When they heard Peter's account of what God had done to explain the transition, they "glorified God" for offering salvation to the Gentiles.

This transition was not without problems, however. When some of the first wave preached Jesus to Greek Gentiles in Antioch and "a great number believed and turned to the Lord", this raised concerns at headquarters. Fortunately, they sent Barnabas to deal with it. When he saw the grace of God flowing through the situation, he rejoiced and joined in, fulfilling his leadership role by exhorting them to cleave unto the Lord with purpose of heart. In other words, it was clear to Barnabas that God was in it, it was consistent with His plan and power, and he simply encouraged them to stick close to the One who loved them, died for them and rose to share life with them forever.

This was good leadership from home base in Jerusalem, working within God's plan to encourage His church as He was developing it. This is how it was supposed to work. God has a good plan, and if we will follow His leading, we can be a part of reaching the world with the wonderful news of Jesus. With Peter's authoritative experience to instruct and Barnabas' encouraging word to uplift, the transition to include ministry to the Gentiles got off to a smooth start, although Paul would have to admonish Peter about it later in Antioch.

. . .

And thus the first wave comes to a close. The 10,000 born and raised in Jerusalem washed over the surrounding countryside, spawning churches throughout the region. The apostles did follow up ministry to empower, establish and encourage those churches. The transition to include the Gentiles took place in a way that even the most orthodox Jews could understand. With God's plan and His power, the church was off to a good start.

Throughout the book of Acts, there are constant references to churches in other cities, which must have resulted from this first wave. By the time Paul had completed his "mother eagle" role, and it was time for his ministry to the Gentiles to begin, the first wave had basically accomplished the first phase of the church as outlined by Jesus at His ascension. There were churches going strong "in Jerusalem, in all Judea, and in Samaria."

Because there was a church in Damascus at the time of Paul's conversion, God could send Ananias to go help Paul understand what had happened to him on the road there and to pass the power on to him. Because there was a church in Antioch, there was a safe incubator where Barnabas could take Paul to learn and gain experience in the Lord and in ministry, a place where they were already ministering to Gentiles. Paul spent a year there, final preparation for his own ministry to the Gentiles.

Ironically, when that time came for Paul to go out, he had to search for places where the Gospel had not already been preached, as that first wave spread across the local area ahead of him. He said his desire was to preach in the "regions beyond", fulfilling his personal mission, not building on "other men's labor" – a clear implication of the great extent of the accomplishments of the first wave. The plan was paying big dividends.

Jesus had made extensive preparations for the church and for "those also which would believe in Him through their word." He provided the power, available to all and transferable to next generation believers, to fulfill the great commission. He arranged for 10,000 recruits to be in Jerusalem for Pentecost, ready to be trained and empowered to go to the world. He moved them out of the nest into a waiting world, with full support from the apostolic home base. He helped them make the transition to include the Gentiles. All the pieces are falling into place, and the plan is progressing nicely, with seedling churches throughout the outlying areas around Jerusalem.

Now it's time for the next phase.

Discussion questions:

1. After Jesus gave the apostles the great commission, why did He tell them to wait before seeking to fulfill it?
2. How did the Lord give the apostles 10,000 helpers to fulfill the great commission?
3. What was the apostle' place and purpose in the early church?
4. How did they fulfill that? And what did the 10,000 learn during the first few weeks of the church?

5. What moved the first wave out of Jerusalem? And why?
6. How much of the world was reached by the first wave? What was the apostles' part?
7. How was transition made to the Gentiles?

CHAPTER 7   PAUL

"...for he is a chosen vessel for Me, to bear My name before the Gentiles, and kings, and the children of Israel..." - Acts 9:15

Although Peter led the disciples in choosing a replacement apostle to take Judas' place, Jesus was way ahead of him, already having someone in mind for the job. This person met all the requirements. He would be personally called by Jesus. He had been a witness to Jesus' life and ministry, as well as His death and resurrection, thus fulfilling the "have been with Me from the beginning" requirement. The fact that he was also a highly trained and respected theologian was an important fringe benefit.

In fact, Paul may have been the only apostle chosen for a particular skill set. Moses had been chosen by God to lead His people out of Egypt because he had a specific skill set learned in the palace of Pharaoh and in the Egyptian army. Paul was chosen because he had a specific skill set learned in the best theological universities of his time, which had perfectly prepared him to lay the theological foundation for the fledgling church, a foundation which would carry it for 2000 years.

Despite the talk that Jesus would build His church upon Peter, He actually built it upon Paul, the apostle "born out of due time."

Although the other apostles were the foundation for the first wave church out of Jerusalem, Paul was the foundation for the church which would be sustainable worldwide for the next two millenniums. Even Peter, who had obviously read some of Paul's letters, refers to "our beloved brother Paul" and "the wisdom given to him", acknowledging Paul's strategic and tactical importance to the developing church.

Ironically, the only thing Jesus refers to specifically when He called Paul to represent Him to the "Gentiles, kings, and the children of Israel" was "how great things he would suffer for My name's sake", perhaps a reference to the suffering inflicted upon His church – "Saul, why are you persecuting Me?" However, he had obviously had His eye on Paul for some time, had been "goading" him for a while, and had a ready answer for, "Lord, what do You want me to do?" His message to Paul through Ananias was one of forgiveness and acceptance and a calling to special service. Jesus had big things in mind for Paul, a critical part for him to play for which he was carefully chosen and for which he would be carefully prepared.

■ ■ ■

Paul was from Tarsus in Celicia, where he had grown up in Gentile territory, unlike the other apostles, who were from the heart of the Jewish homeland. Because of this, Paul may have been more comfortable with ministry to the Gentiles, despite his classic Jewish education in Jerusalem, where he came face to face with Jesus. Consistently identifying himself in public as a Roman indicated an ease with Gentiles which would have facilitated ministry throughout the Roman Empire. Having already made that adjustment as a boy meant he didn't have to make it as a Jewish adult before he could freely relate to the vast Gentile world.

Paul had his life planned out, a life of zealous service to God. He had the preparation to go with the passion, a solid theological education at the finest Jewish universities. Perhaps this was why he was only a casual observer of the Messianic stirring around Jerusalem, as Jesus didn't fit into Paul's plan; or at least he thought He didn't. Paul pressed on diligently with his own plan until he came face to face with Jesus again and found that their plans meshed perfectly – Paul's background, passion and preparation lined up with Jesus' plan for the church as though they were made for each other.

As Paul spent time with Jesus in the wilderness after his conversion, he found that Jesus had the same passion for serving God and that His power joined with Paul's preparation to make an ideal combination. When Jesus told Paul that his mission was to go to the Gentiles, it made sense to him. He easily understood that the other apostles would operate out of their Jerusalem base while he would take on the world. That assignment must have seemed natural, since he saw himself as a citizen of the world, not merely identified with Jerusalem.

■ ■ ■

We have already seen how Jesus worked with Paul to establish an intimate relationship with him and to help him understand His plan and His power. He also worked with him to establish him emotionally; so he would be fully prepared for the "great things he must suffer for My name's sake". As He works with Paul to that end, He passes on to us the foundation for our emotional stability in a difficult world.

In Acts 16, He miraculously delivered him; so Paul could fearlessly face tough things ahead. Following a training session of mob persecution, judicial injustice and a night in a Roman jail, ending in rescue by earthquake and opportunity to share the Gospel with the jailer and his family, Paul would never fear what might happen to him while he was in the Lord's service. In fact, his summary of the incident demonstrates its effect upon him – "after we had suffered and were shamefully entreated at Philippi, we were bold in our God to speak the Gospel" in Thessalonica, thankful to be "allowed of God to be put in trust with the Gospel." This is emotional stability in the face of affliction, something he obviously passed on to the Thessalonians, as he commended them for it, as well.

In 2 Corinthians 12, Paul records how Jesus helped him with his pride and reminded him that His grace was sufficient for him; so he could not only deal with infirmities, but glory in them. This was a tough lesson for a strong independent man like Paul to learn, but having learned to rely on Christ alone, rather than upon his limited human strength, he went on in ministry, knowing all things would work together for good as he followed God's plan. This lesson was critical to Paul's stability in ministry, a lesson he passed on to the church to stabilize them, as well.

In Philippians 4, Paul shares how he has learned to be content in every situation, because he can do all things through Christ who strengthens him. The only way to *learn* that lesson was to experience difficult things and see the Lord provide, strengthen and bring him through. This prepared him to face the litany of trials and tribulations listed in 2 Corinthians 11 which would overwhelm the normal man. Jesus knew that strength in the inner man would be critical for Paul's mission, and so ministered to Paul in such a way as to build that calmness and strength in him.

As Paul was troubled, yet not distressed; perplexed, but not in despair; persecuted, but not forsaken; cast down, but not destroyed, he gained a deeper understanding of his weakness (earthen vessel) and of the greatness of God's power (the power that raised Jesus from the dead). He became more and more settled and sure, keeping his eyes not on the things which are seen, but on the things which are not seen, seeing God's grace in the toughest situations. He became more focused on the fact that Jesus was with him than on the difficulties he faced. That fact lifted him, providing him the buoyancy he needed to weather the storms.

All this Jesus did as He prepared Paul to lead the second wave. He needed a man who not only had the theological training and a personal relationship with the Savior, but the emotional stability to carry him through the "great things he would suffer for My name's sake." Jesus never does things halfway. If He was going to send an ambassador to represent Him "before the Gentiles and kings and the children of Israel", He would obviously take great pains to fully prepare him for everything he would have to face.

Since Jesus was the One who knew what Paul would have to face, He knew how to prepare him. As He took him through those different stages of training, He also took him through the early stages of his mission to the world. And as Jesus laid the foundation for Paul's life and ministry, He laid the foundation for the church. The emotional stability things He taught Paul, Paul passed on to the church, even as he was laying the theological foundation which would carry the church for 2000 years. Now we see how that preparation paid off, as Paul leads the second wave, and the church spreads beyond "Jerusalem, Judea and Samaria" into "the uttermost part of the earth".

Discussion questions:

1. What skill set did Paul possess when Jesus called him to be an apostle?
2. What is the rationale for saying Jesus built the church upon Paul, rather than Peter?
3. What was it about Paul's background which made him the perfect ambassador to the Gentiles?
4. Explain how Jesus built emotional stability into Paul's experience and ministry.
5. Explain how Paul passed that on to the church.
6. Explain how the foundation Jesus laid in Paul's life laid the foundation for the church, as well.
7. Summarize the special training Jesus gave Paul.

CHAPTER 8   SECOND WAVE

"...being confident of this very thing, that He who has begun a good work in you will complete it until the day of Jesus Christ..."
- Philippians 1:6

We would hardly recognize Paul's missionary method in our day of highly organized, extensively financed, time intensive missionary work. And yet Paul and his network of fellow laborers of the second wave reached much of the world of their time following the plan and utilizing the power. Their method was deceptively simple, relying completely upon God's involvement and on the life-changing power of the gospel. Paul would go to a city; locate interested people; share the gospel; help establish them in the faith with competent local leadership; commit them to God's care, and then move on for a repeat performance in the next city. Meanwhile, his fellow laborers would do follow up work or continue to share the Gospel in their city, often hosting a church in their house.

Paul understood from the start that this was not a human endeavor, but was entirely dependent upon the plan and the power of God. He outlined this in 1 Corinthians, chapter 2, where he says that he did not come with "excellence of speech or of wisdom," knowing only one thing – "Jesus Christ, and Him crucified." He understood that it was not about "enticing words of man's wisdom, but in demonstration of the Spirit and of power." Thus his "weakness, fear and much trembling" was not a problem, but even an asset, that their faith should stand not "in the wisdom of men, but in the power of God." Paul was committed to having the church begun in the proper relationship with Jesus, the Head of the church, totally dependent on His grace, power and sustenance. Anything less would simply be a new religion.

There didn't even seem to be a standard time required. Often it was a few months. Sometimes it was an extremely short visit. Sometimes Paul spent a little more time – a year and a half in Corinth and three years in Ephesus, for example. He relied on the gospel – "the power of God to salvation." It seemed that if the seed took, producing genuine fruit, Paul spent time establishing them in the faith and then trusted them to the Lord's care, fully acknowledging that it was Christ's church and therefore **His** responsibility. Paul's responsibility was to share the gospel. He laid the foundation for a sustainable church. Then he moved on.

He basically followed the "planting and watering" concept he mentioned later. In Iconium, for example, Paul and Barnabas "planted" among both Jews and Gentiles. They stayed there quite a while, "speaking boldly in the Lord", who also bore witness to the word of His grace with signs and wonders. However, when persecution arose, and their lives were in danger, they moved on.

They later returned to "water" the seed they had planted. On their way back to Antioch, they stopped at Iconium to "strengthen the souls of the disciples, exhorting them to continue in the faith," in spite of persecution. They appointed elders in every church, prayed with them and commended them to the Lord. Then they left the Lord to care for His church while they went on to share the Gospel elsewhere.

In the meantime, these young churches were continually on Paul's mind and in his prayers. So after he had represented them at the council in Jerusalem, making the case for their equality with Jewish believers, he determined to visit them again to see how they were doing. Although a disagreement with Barnabas broke up that team, Paul pressed on, asking Silas to go with him as he revisited his ministry in different cities, "confirming the churches." The result of this format was that the churches were "established in the faith and increased in number daily."

. . .

And Paul always had his eye on "the regions beyond" – the next city which needed the Gospel – always aware of the great commission and his responsibility within that framework. Some Spirit-led restless energy constantly kept him on the move – the world was waiting – to the point that in his letter to the Romans he shared his plans to go to Spain. Therefore, whether he was comfortably ensconced in a teaching position in the growing church at Antioch or confirming new churches in outlying areas, he was always looking to go into more of the world the Lord had asked them to reach, always relying upon the leading of the Holy Spirit, so he could stay within the plan and the power.

When he and Silas were "forbidden by the Holy Spirit to preach the word in Asia and prevented from going into Bithynia," they waited until a vision assured them that "the Lord had called them to preach the gospel in Macedonia." There they found a group waiting to hear, stayed at Lydia's bed and breakfast, and shared in the birth of the church in Thyatira, a church Jesus takes to heart, following up personally in His messages to the churches in Revelation.

Although Paul and Silas suffered in the jail in Philippi, God's supporting power broke them out, and another group of believers was formed around the jailer's family. We can only imagine how this group took root and grew. But we do know that when Paul wrote to them later, they consisted of "all the saints in Christ Jesus who were in Philippi, with the bishops and deacons" in whom Paul was confident that "He who had begun a good work in them would continue it until the day of Jesus Christ." When the Word takes root according to God's plan and in His power, a sustainable church results.

■ ■ ■

When the Spirit finally did take Paul to preach the word in Asia, he worked out of a base camp in Ephesus. Following up with a group of disciples of John the Baptist, Paul introduced them to the One whom John had said would come after him. They were baptized in the name of Jesus and were filled with the Spirit. Then Paul ministered in the local synagogue for three months until some unbelieving Jews ran him off.

So he moved with the believing Jews to a new location – "the school of Tyrannus" – where he ministered the word of the Lord for three years. During this time, all those who lived in Asia, both Jews and Greeks, heard the word of the Lord Jesus. God also did His part during that time, doing miracles by the hand of Paul and dealing with a Jewish exorcist in a way which caused fear to fall upon the inhabitants of Ephesus, and the name of the Lord Jesus was magnified.

So, as Paul did his part in the plan, and God demonstrated His power in support, the Gospel reached all of Asia. Many who believed came confessing their sins in repentance, and they burned over

50,000 pieces of silver's worth of magic books as a demonstration of their turning from their old way of life. So the word of the Lord "grew mightily and prevailed." This whole section of the world heard the Gospel and responded as the second wave moved out from the Jerusalem area into the Gentile world.

Paul was a good "father" to his spiritual offspring, taking his responsibility extremely seriously, despite the persecutions which shortened his time with them. Although he was just passing through Troas, he stayed up all night instructing the church there, and healed the young man who went to sleep during that long night, fell out a window and died. He then called together at his regional base camp in Ephesus all the church leaders, probably from all of Asia, and spent significant time with them giving them final instructions, as he would never see them again. Only then did he pray with them and commend them "to God and to the word of His grace."

Paul did this same thing in other places he passed through. Traveling on, he spent seven days with disciples in Tyre, teaching and praying with them. In Caesarea, he stopped at Philip's house to encourage him and his family in their ministry. Paul did his part thoroughly and conscientiously and then he trusted young churches to the Lord, whose ultimate responsibility the church was.

■ ■ ■

Then it appeared that God put Paul out to pasture – two years in house arrest in Caesarea and two years in Rome. In Caesarea, Felix, the governor, kept him bound and talked with him often, hoping for a bribe. In the meantime, Paul was free to receive visitors. There is no real explanation for this four year hiatus, but perhaps the young church and Paul's network of co-laborers were ready to stand on their own and needed time to learn further dependence on the Lord Himself, rather than on Paul,

He went to work at his final forward operating base – Rome – transported at government expense, which enabled him to share the Gospel at Malta and encourage brethren and be encouraged by them at Puteoli, Appii Forum and Three Inns on the way. In Rome he ministered under house arrest, sharing the Gospel first with local Jewish leaders. When there was a disagreement among them about what Paul was saying, he turned his attention to the Gentiles.

It's interesting that God's plan took Paul to the center of the Roman Empire, the place that gave maximum access to the world through government maintained travel and communications systems. As Paul had the freedom to receive anyone at his own rented house, multitudes of people stopped to see him as they came from all over the world to do business in Rome. Paul openly ministered there for two years, "preaching the kingdom of God and teaching the things which concern the Lord Jesus Christ with all confidence, no one forbidding him." He ministered the Gospel in the palace of Caesar himself, as he indicates in his greetings from those of Caesar's household in one of his letters.

Paul also carried out his worldwide church administrative duties from this communication center. He received messengers from outlying churches as they came with questions for him and also with provisions to meet his needs. The majority of Paul's epistles were written from Rome, responding to those churches, addressing those questions and building the theological base which would sustain them and the growing church for 2000 years.

Rome was a fitting culmination of Paul's ministry, a place to preach the Gospel to a constant stream of the citizens of the world, who would take the Gospel home with them. It was the perfect place to follow up with the growing church throughout the world. And it was the ideal location for overseeing his network of co-laborers through correspondence and as they traveled in and out of Rome. God's plan was working to perfection, and His power would carry it on through the future.

■ ■ ■

Although Paul was the leader of this second wave, there were others who worked with him; some even trained by Paul, who often get lost in the shuffle, the limelight of Paul's well-known missionary journeys. We have already met Barnabas and Silas, team mates critical to Paul's ministry. When Paul and Barnabas split up, Barnabas continued his ministry with a new team mate. But there were others who were just as important to this second wave which took the Gospel to the world in this first generation of the church.

Aquila and Priscilla took Paul in at Corinth, worked with him, learned from him, were discipled by him. They were so well trained by Paul that when an eloquent, earnest young preacher by the name of Apollos came to town teaching the baptism of John, they took him in and passed on what they had learned from Paul. Aquila and Priscilla's ministry transformed Apollos' ministry, and he went on to be a powerful preacher of the Gospel who had a major impact in the second wave. And there were others who Paul trained and added to the team which would fulfill the great commission.

In Lystra, Paul found "a certain disciple" named Timothy who had come to faith through his mother and his grandmother and was "well spoken of" by the local brethren. Paul took him under his wing, and he traveled with Paul for a while, listening, learning, growing in the faith. Then Paul gave him leadership responsibility at the church in Ephesus, to keep them on track; and Ephesus was the hub of a wider ministry in that area. Paul's instructions to him indicate the responsibility he carried as he led the church and took part in the great commission.

Timothy was charged to stand "strong in the grace that is in Christ Jesus," the only basis for successful ministry. He was urged to "hold fast the pattern of sound words" which he heard from Paul, and, by the power of the Holy Spirit, to keep "that good thing which was committed to Him." Paul had obviously invested a lot in Timothy, and now he asked him to pass that along to "faithful men who will be able to teach others also." Paul asked him to train others, to ordain other leaders according to careful guidelines Paul laid out, and to supervise their ministry as he continued his own.

Paul also reminded Timothy to "do the work of an evangelist," to reach his corner of the world, and thus "fulfill his ministry." Even though Paul expected Timothy to lead the church in the larger area around Ephesus, he reminded him to always be aware of the great commission, as that was the whole point of the emerging church. Therefore, Timothy always did the work of an evangelist and trained others to go and do the same.

And then there was Epaphras in Colosse, whom Paul characterized as a faithful minister of Christ who taught them "the word of the truth of the Gospel" and "the grace of God in truth." This resulted in a report to Paul of their "faith in Christ Jesus and their love for all the saints." Paul writes to them as an established church, established by someone other than Paul.

Paul goes on to say that while Epaphras was visiting him in prison, he was "always laboring fervently for them in prayer, that they may stand perfect and complete in all the will of God," a beautiful picture of a pastor's heart. Paul also said that Epaphras had "a great zeal for those in Laodicea and Hierapolis," an obvious reference to his passion for the great commission, as well. It's compatriots like these who contributed to the second wave extending the Gospel to the ends of the earth.

Then, of course, there's Titus, commissioned to care for the church in Crete. Paul reminded him to speak with authority that "the grace of God that brings salvation has appeared to all; that Jesus "gave Himself for us, that He might redeem us;" and that we are to "adorn the doctrine of God our Savior in all things." Obviously, Titus was to provide leadership for the church in Crete in such a way that the Gospel was spread throughout that island, keeping the great commission always in mind.

And don't forget Mark. He went with Paul and Barnabas on their first missionary journey and learned much before going home midjourney. Although Paul was not sure about taking him the next time, and that issue caused a split with Barnabas, Mark went with Barnabas to minister in Cyprus. Later, Paul asked Timothy to bring Mark to him, as he was "useful to [Paul] for ministry." So Mark must have developed into a competent fellow laborer under Barnabas' tutelage, as well as from his experiences on the first trip.

There are several others that Paul mentions in passing who have helped him or are helping him, people who are also active in this second wave. There was Tychicus, "a beloved brother, faithful minister, and fellow servant in the Lord," who Paul sent to Ephesus. There was Nymphas and the church in his house, apparently in Laodicea. There was Archippus, who was encouraged to "take heed to the ministry which he had received in the Lord, that he may fulfill it." There was Justus, a "fellow worker for the kingdom of God." There was Artemas, who Paul felt was competent to take Titus' place on Crete. Paul also mentions Zenas, the lawyer, who would be a help to the brethren. Then there were thirty-four men and women, from Phoebe to Quartus, who Paul mentioned in the last chapter of Romans as those who had labored with him in the Lord.

Philemon, Apphia, Aristarchus, Demas and Luke show up in the book of Philemon, along with the aforementioned Archippus, Epaphras and Mark. Onesiphorus, Erastus, Trophimus, Eubulus, Pudens, Linus and Claudia show up in 2 Timothy, along with the aforementioned Priscilla and Aquila. Lucius, Jason, Sosipater and Tertius show up in Romans, along with the aforementioned Timothy. Stephanas, Fortunatus and Achaicus show up in the book of 1 Corinthians, along with the aforementioned Timothy, Apollos and Priscilla and Aquila. In Philippians, Paul mentions Euodias, Syntyche, Clement, Epaphroditus, "those women who labored with me in the Gospel" and other "fellow laborers, whose names are in the book of life."

Paul also involved people in praying for him, making them feel part of his ministry. He asked the Thessalonians to pray for him, "that the word of the Lord may have free course and be glorified...and that they might be delivered from unreasonable and wicked men..." He asked the Ephesians to pray for him "that utterance may be given unto me, that I may open my mouth boldly, to make known the mystery of the gospel..." Paul always saw his ministry as teamwork with his network of helpers or prayer helpers.

Therefore, as Paul went from city to city preaching the Gospel he also built a leadership team to work with him and without him (when he moved on) to help fulfill the great commission. He understood his roles of evangelist and administrator as the second wave spread across the world. He passed on what Jesus had committed to him; so the emerging church could be thriving and sustainable long after his work was done. Then he followed it all up carefully, as we will see in the next chapter.

Discussion questions:

1. Why do we designate Paul as the leader of the second wave?
2. Give a simple description of Paul's church planting method, and explain why it worked.
3. How do we know that the great commission was always on Paul's heart?
4. List several deciding factors which determined the length of time Paul might spend in any given city.
5. Summarize Paul's network building method.
6. List some of Paul's better known co-laborers. Some of his lesser known ones.
7. Why did God send Paul to Rome to conclude his ministry?

CHAPTER 9　　　　PAUL: FOLLOW UP

"Therefore, my beloved brethren, be steadfast, immovable, always abounding in the work of the Lord..." - 1 Corinthians 15:58

I n our age of instant worldwide communication, it's hard to imagine the obstacles facing Paul as he was trying to hold the burgeoning church together. It's truly amazing to think that when it was difficult to get a message across town, Paul was able to keep in touch with fledgling churches clear across the Roman Empire in a meaningful way. Somehow he was able to hear how they were doing and address their needs in a timely fashion, which helped those churches stay on track and progress in the right direction.

We have already examined some of Paul's follow up ministry on his missionary journeys as he revisited churches he had planted earlier. Now we look more closely at those visits and at the point and the purpose of Paul's letters to young churches who were just getting started in a hostile world. To facilitate the latter, Rome was the ideal location – a communication center connected with the entire Roman Empire. It also helped him stay in touch with his network of co-laborers as they shared in his follow up ministry to the new churches.

The foundation for Paul's follow up ministry was his prayer ministry, counting first and foremost upon the Lord's concern for **His** church. So often in his letters he tells them he has been praying for them, seeking God's best for them. In his letter to the Colossians he gives us an outline of his concerns, which I'm sure he feels for all the churches under his care. He prays for those things which will strengthen and guide them and help them grow and prosper in their ministry.

He prays for them that they may be filled with the knowledge of God's will in all wisdom and spiritual understanding, reminding them that God Himself is ready to lead them and watch over them. He prays they may walk worthy of the Lord, being fruitful and increasing in the knowledge of God, reminding them that their lives have a purpose, and they should be moving into it. And he prays that they may be strengthened by God's glorious power all the way to patience and perseverance with joyfulness, reminding them that life is tough, but the Lord cares and will see them through as they look to Him.

■ ■ ■

Paul's follow up visits were intended to carry the churches far into the future, as we see in his final visit to Ephesus. He reminded them of all that he had been and had taught them in his church planting time with them, in spite of all the trials they had faced together. He reminded them, Jews and Gentiles, that he had shared with them publicly and from house to house everything they would need to know concerning "repentance toward God and faith toward our Lord Jesus Christ" – "the whole counsel of God."

He admonished the leaders to take heed to themselves and to the flock which was their responsibility, "to feed the church of God, which He has purchased with His own blood." He warned them of dangers ahead, "grievous wolves entering in among them" and some of their own "speaking perverse things, to draw away disciples after them." He reminded them of his investment among them "night and day with tears." Then he "commended them to God, and to the word of His grace, which was able to build them up, and to give them an inheritance among all them who are sanctified." Finally, he prayed with them all before leaving.

Paul did this over and over as he revisited his church plants, firming up and finalizing his ministry and confirming the churches. He established local leaders in their ministry, transferring responsibility to them and admonishing them to look to the Lord and His word in fulfilling it. He encouraged them, prayed with them and commended them to the care of the Lord, the Head of the church and the One who would watch over them when he left. This was the final step in the "planting and watering" process, confirming the work that had been done before leaving it with the Lord.

■ ■ ■

Then, although Paul might not see them again, he kept in touch through his communication network and through letters, hearing their problems and questions and responding. He was amazingly close and caring with his "children" spread throughout the empire. He prayed for them always, kept track of them and addressed their needs.

He knew about the discord between Jews and Gentiles in Rome and about their lack of understanding about their new life in Christ.

So he explained in detail what God had done in and through the Jews and pointed out how they needed, along with the Gentiles, to trust in Christ alone, the fulfillment of promises made to Abraham. He explained how they all needed to give up any trust in the flesh and walk in the Spirit in newness of life. Then he explained how they should relate to the world and to each other in this new status, so they could move beyond their differences into a long term lifestyle which would establish and sustain the church.

He knew about the carnal condition of the Corinthians and about their misunderstanding of the gifts of the Spirit. Reminding them of his love for them, he discusses their condition, including some very personal observations, and calls upon them to make adjustments (and is blessed by their zealous response to his admonitions). He gives them guidance concerning the gifts of the Spirit and their proper uses and reminds them of the priority of love. He reminds them of all that they have in the death and resurrection of Jesus and encourages them also to walk in newness of life. He closes with a summary of his relationship with the Lord and a defense of his apostleship before calling them to follow his example and heed his edification.

He knew the Galatians had gotten caught up in debate between the law and grace which hindered their further growth into the joy of the Lord. So he addresses that problem at length, admonishing them to stand fast in the liberty wherewith Christ has made them free, to serve one another in love, and to plant good things so they can reap good things. Then he encourages them also to walk in newness of life. Again, he addresses specific needs in the church while calling them to a loving, sustainable lifestyle which will carry them far into the future.

Paul had spent three years in Ephesus, teaching, preaching and establishing the church there; so his letter to the Ephesians has a different flavor and feel. He begins with a tone of familiarity and fellowship, using the term "we" generously, including himself in their experience with the Lord. He's thankful for their faith and love and tells them that he is praying for them.

He reminds them of their calling in the Lord and of their regeneration-by-grace experience which made them His workmanship, created for good works. He reviews how they, as Gentiles, are now fellow citizens with the saints, built on "the foundation of the apostles and prophets, Jesus Christ himself being the chief cornerstone." He wants them to understand the fullness of that status and to maintain their unity there. He admonishes them to grow together, "speaking the truth in love," putting off the old way and putting on the new.

Encouraging them to walk in love, he goes on to give rather detailed instructions for each part of their new life, from marriage and family to work situations. He closes with reminders about how tough life can be, and encourages them to put on "the whole armor of God." He ends with a blessing and tells them he will send someone to let them know how he is doing, another act of fellowship. This is obviously a letter of loving care, not simply one of theology, although we benefit from the abundance of theology contained therein. When we put this letter into the perspective of Paul's long term ministry at Ephesus, we learn more about his follow up ministry to all his churches.

■ ■ ■

In stark contrast to his three years at Ephesus, Paul only spent a matter of days at Thessalonica; but they were intense days which apparently forged an incredible bond between him and the Thessalonians. With a reputation as one who had "turned the world upside down" and had "suffered...shamefully...at Philippi," Paul was bold to preach the Gospel "in power and in the Holy Ghost and in much assurance" at Thessalonica. This apparently added weight to his words, because the nucleus of the new church there received it "not as the word of men, but as it is in truth, the word of God, which effectually works in those who believe."

The result was equally intense. Those Thessalonian believers became followers of Paul and Silas and of the Lord, having received the word in the midst of much affliction – Paul's hosts were hauled before the rulers of the city, and Paul and Silas were sent out of town by the brethren, for their safety – and with joy of the Holy Ghost. They "became examples to all who believe in Macedonia and Achaia," and their testimony and the word of the Lord spread from there, not only in Macedonia and Achaia, but preceded Paul and Silas as they moved on. Everywhere they went, people told Paul and Silas how the Thessalonians had "turned to God from idols to serve the living and true God; and to wait for His Son from heaven, whom He raised from the dead, even Jesus, who delivered us from the wrath to come." Talk about intense, but because it didn't depend on human energy or wisdom, but on the power of God, a vital church was planted in Thessalonica in that brief, intense time.

With the background of that kind of relationship, how did Paul follow up in his letter to them? He begins with thanksgiving and prayer, telling them how he treasures the memory of their time together, constantly remembering their "work of faith, labor of love, and patience of hope in our Lord Jesus Christ," which gives him confidence that God has something special in mind for them – "knowing, brethren beloved, your election of God." He goes on to remind them of his heartfelt care for them, how he was gentle, cherishing, willing to give them, "not the gospel of God only, but also our own souls, because you were dear to us." He also reminds them that he treated them as his children, "exhorting, comforting and charging every one of you," and thus expecting them to "walk worthy of God," wishing he could see them again, hearing that they desired to see him again, too. He calls them his "hope, his joy, his crown of rejoicing…his comfort in all our affliction and distress." This is heart-to-heart stuff we don't find in other letters, but what encouraging thoughts for them to rest in as they face their own tribulations.

He shares his love for them and his heart's desire for them, that they may "increase and abound in love one toward another and toward all, even as we do toward you." He shares his desire for the Lord to "establish their hearts unblameable in holiness before God," his way of saying he wants God's best for them, and encourages them to continue to move toward maturity in love and in their new life. And he is thankful for Timothy's good report of their faith and love and wishes he could see them and "perfect that which is lacking in their faith." What a beautiful picture of a father's care for his "children," something which must have been a great encouragement to individuals and the church.

Perhaps as a result of the afflictions they shared or of the tribulations they are enduring, he offers them the hope of Christ's imminent return, although he tells them we don't know when. He encourages them to walk as children of the light, putting on spiritual armor. He gives them a bullet point list of the facets of new life, reminds them that God is faithful to preserve them "blameless unto the coming of our Lord Jesus Christ," and commends them to His care.

When he writes again, he is encouraged that their faith has grown exceedingly, that their love abounds and that they are patient in persecution and tribulation; which indicates that he has kept track of them. He clarifies the misunderstanding they had about Christ's coming and gives further details about it to comfort them. He reminds them of God's faithfulness and of his confidence in them. He addresses a couple of minor problems in the church and then closes with a blessing of peace for them from "the Lord of peace Himself."

Paul poured out his heart for them and put his life on the line in the brief time he was in Thessalonica. He speaks to them on that same level when he writes to them. The result is a church which is faithful and strong even in the face of tribulation, a church which is maturing and growing, and a church which has a wide influence throughout their region, impacting their whole area with the Gospel. This is the kind of impact Paul had as he planted churches and followed up with them through letters and through his communication network.

■ ■ ■

And then there's his letter to Colosse, where Epaphras had planted a church and then had come to report the results to Paul – "saints and faithful brethren" with faith in Christ and love for all the saints. It's worthy of note that Epaphras came to Paul, rather than to Jerusalem and the apostles and other church leaders. This is an interesting acknowledgement of Paul's leadership in the worldwide church, both from Epaphras' point of view and from Paul's, who then thought it important to write to the Colossians to give them an official foundation for their faith and new life.

Although this was characteristic of all Paul's letters to a certain extent, his letter to the Colossians was very definitely a complete summary of the Christian faith and of their responsibilities within it. He begins with a thankful prayer for all they have received through Christ from the Father – "deliverance from the power of darkness and translation into the kingdom of His dear Son." He summarizes all that that means and encourages them to grow toward maturity in their relationship with Him – "Christ in you, the hope of glory."

He warns them about those who would try to lead them astray through philosophies and traditions of this world, and admonishes them to "walk in Christ, rooted and built up in Him...for in Him dwells all the fullness of the Godhead bodily, and you are complete in Him." He calls them to newness of life, the resurrection life, leaving behind the old life. He gives a beautiful description of what their corporate life should be like – kindness, humbleness, forgiveness, bound together by love, the peace of God and thankfulness; letting "the word of Christ dwell in them richly in all wisdom;" ministering to each other in song; and doing everything "in the name of the Lord Jesus." Any church would do well to follow those guidelines, but they were obviously designed to carry the Colossian church far into the future.

Then he gives them detailed instructions for how their new lifestyle should work in marriage, family and work situations. He asks them to pray for him, tying them into the wider church family, and tells them Tychicus is coming from that wider church family to help them. He closes by introducing them to others in that family, speaks well of their pastor, Epaphras, and has encouraging words for two others of their number, Nymphas and Archippus. He asks them to share his letter with another church and to read the letter he sent to them, further tying them into the church at large.

It is most instructive to consider this letter to a church which Paul did not plant, but for which he assumes instructional responsibility. He wants to make sure they have the same theological foundation and practical direction as all the other newborn churches. And he helps them take their place in the wider church, understanding that there will be interaction between them and other churches and between them and other co-laborers of Paul as they pass through their city. This is a beautiful example of Paul laying the groundwork for a sustainable church which would be equipped for progress, growth and outreach far into the future.

These letters to specific churches, addressing specific needs, were the bulk of the foundation for the newborn church worldwide. This foundation was filled out by letters from Peter, John, James and Jude out of the base camp at Jerusalem, letters addressed to the church at large – "the twelve tribes which are scattered abroad," "the strangers scattered," "my little children," and "those who are sanctified by God the Father and preserved in Jesus Christ and called." And then there's the summary of the deeper theology – the letter to the Hebrews – addressed in general to the "holy brethren," to those who "have become partakers of Christ." The letter ends with a far reaching admonition – "run with patience the race that is set before you, looking to Jesus" – and an encouraging, supportive benediction – "May the God of peace who brought up our Lord Jesus from the dead, that great Shepherd of the sheep, through the blood of the everlasting covenant, make you complete in every good work to do His will, working in you that which is well pleasing in His sight, through Jesus Christ, to whom be glory forever and ever, Amen."

This completed foundation not only met the needs of the early church but held and sustained the resulting worldwide church for 2000 years. Beyond the early church, these same letters are what we build on today. They are part of the plan to take the Gospel to the world, both then and now.

■ ■ ■

Then there was the ministry of Paul's network of co-laborers who picked up where Paul left off in specific locations, maintaining contact with Paul as they did so. Their names and ministries are interspersed throughout Paul's letters as we watch them do their part and keep in touch with him as they provide communications between the churches and Paul. These men are vital to the sustainable life of the growing church. Their names were mentioned in the last chapter, but now we look a little deeper.

Titus, who Paul called "my own son after the common faith," is a good example. Apparently, Paul led him to the Lord and he traveled some with Paul, learning and growing. And when Crete needed oversight, Paul left Titus there, to "set in order things that are wanting." He gave him specific instructions and trusted him to carry them out and establish the church in Crete, and he followed that up with a letter. But that was only a temporary assignment. Paul expected him to join him in Nicopolis for the winter after Artemas or Tychicus arrived to take his place. Paul also sent him to Dalmatia to help with the church there, making the best use of good people. Titus also went to Corinth for Paul; and when he brought back a good report, it was as encouraging to Titus as it was to Paul, another example of Paul's leadership development style.

Most of us are vaguely familiar with Timothy, and in the last chapter we learned of his responsibility to the church in the larger metropolitan area around Ephesus, but there was more, as Paul sought to use him to the greater profit of other churches. He sent him to help out in Corinth. He sent him to help out in Thessalonica, to report back and then was included in the opening greeting in Paul's letter to that church. He was also included in the opening greeting in Paul's letter to the Philippians, which may indicate some kind of ministry to that church. Apparently, he was kind of a right hand man to Paul.

Paul sent him two letters to encourage him and to keep him on track, in one of which he encouraged him to pass on what he had learned from Paul "to faithful men who will be able to teach others also." This is what Paul expected from his "great commission network," as he trained them to train others, as well.

Apollos was also sent to help out in Corinth. Tychicus was sent to Ephesus and to Colosse to report from Paul, "comfort their hearts," and report back to Paul. Epaphroditus came from Philippi to report to Paul on the status of the church there. Silvanus appears in the opening greeting of Paul's letter to the Thessalonians, apparently involved in ministry there.

We have already established that Paul was the leader of the second wave and the administrator of the worldwide church, but now we see that he knew that he could not do it alone. So he not only gathered and trained a network of co-laborers, he directed their ministry in following up his work in the church. Paul was not only reaching the world with the Gospel, he was building the church of the future.

Discussion questions:

1. Why was being in Rome important for Paul's follow up ministry?
2. What was the foundation for that ministry? Give a summary of his concerns.
3. What was the purpose of Paul's follow up visits, besides his immediate concerns?
   Explain how he accomplished that.
4. How do we know that Paul knew the problems of individual churches as he writes to them?

5. What was different about Paul's follow up with the Ephesians? And why?

6. What's the reason for all the heart-to-heart stuff in Paul's follow up with the Thessalonians? And what was the result?

7. What does the letter to the Colossians tell us about Paul's leadership in the worldwide church and his responsibility for its future?

8. How did Paul recruit, train, establish and utilize his "great commission network" of co- laborers to plant, water and confirm the church and prepare it for the future?

CHAPTER 10   2000 YEARS

"...lo, I am with you always, even to the end of the age."
- Matthew 28:20

So, how did a despised religion of outcasts and slaves survive and thrive? How did 120 ordinary people gathered in the upper room waiting for the power become a worldwide church which not only survived, but grew and thrived for 2000 years? How did weak earthen vessels reach the world each successive generation with the same good news that Jesus gave the apostles, with the same results? And how was all this accomplished in a dark and fallen world which was consistently antagonistic to the Gospel?

As we consider God's plan and His power, the answers to the above questions become obvious. The church was not a human endeavor, planned and implemented with the best that people could put together. This was a supernatural undertaking, emanating from the mind and heart of God Himself. God took ordinary people, endowed them with supernatural life and power, and even the "gates of hell" could not withstand them. This is a whole other equation for church planting, and, as such, is not surprising that it did so well for so long.

As we think about the book of Acts and the birth of the church, we have a tendency to focus on the short term – the first century and the early church – and see it as an isolated part of church history. But God's plan was designed as a long term plan, intended to reach the world for 2000 years. Therefore, all the elements of that plan were designed to work for 2000 years, as fresh and sustainable as when Jesus first set them in motion.

God knew that the plan was not simply for the first century; so He planned accordingly. Jesus knew that the plan was not simply for the first century; so He taught and prepared and trained accordingly. The Holy Spirit knew that the plan was not simply for the first century; so He empowered the early church planters with power that was easily and completely transferable; so that each succeeding generation for 2000 years would be able to carry out their mission in spite of human weaknesses.

The early church was not just experimental church – trial and error to figure out what would work best. Although it took a little while to overspread the region, it always was full blown church, designed by God to not only reach the world in the first generation, but to reproduce itself fully sustainable for generations to come. They were simply implementing the plan, not just trying to figure out a plan.

■ ■ ■

This also becomes a great encouragement for us in the work which is ahead of us as a church. When we think of His long-range plan, announced and carried out since the beginning, we can count on it and work with it as we move into the future. The plan which has worked so well for 2000 years is surely good for whatever we have to face. The real question is whether or not we will work that plan or insist on our own. Any church growth seminar which does not focus first on His plan will fall far short of what God has in mind for the contemporary church, no matter how exciting it may appear.

As we have watched the under girding and enabling of His power throughout history, we can go forward with confidence for what He has given us to do. To question the sufficiency of the power given to build and to sustain the church is to question the Person of God Himself. Once again, the real question is whether or not we will rely on that power or insist on trusting our own. Any church growth seminar which does not focus first on that power leaves us to do the best we can in our own strength, which will always peter out after a while, leaving no lasting impact.

Jesus made good preparations for His church. He had the perfect plan for a sustainable church which would continually reach the world with the good news that God was available and wanted to share our lives. He personally laid a solid foundation for the beginning and the continuing of a newborn church in a hostile world. Long term, sustainable, transferable power was made available so that the weakest earthen vessels throughout the history of the world could effectively carry out that plan.

Despite our attempts to come up with a better plan and improved methods, the old plan with its power is still the only proven way for genuine church growth and sustainability. God still knows those who are His, and He is still calling them. He is still asking those of us who know the Savior to bear witness, empowered by His Spirit. He is still using earthen vessels; so we don't have to be responsible for generating the power necessary to make it all work. The only time we have problems is when we get off track and begin to rely on ourselves.

■ ■ ■

Jesus jump started the church at Pentecost; so they hit the ground running – 10,000 strong. Although the job seemed impossible when given to twelve or even 120, when the rest of the church showed up to help fulfill the great commission, it seemed much more doable, especially since the risen Savior was so obviously and personally involved. Then it became a logical extension of His ministry, not simply a tough job dumped into the lap of the newborn church. And they reached into most of the known world within their lifetime, as evidenced by the following.

The plan and its attendant power worked so well and so quickly that deep into Paul's ministry of worldwide outreach, when he wrote his first letter to the Corinthians, there were still living many witnesses to the resurrection, referenced in chapter 15 in Paul's proof that Jesus rose from the dead. Thus, it is obvious that much of the world was reached before that first generation of the church had died, an amazing feat possible only by the power of God in support of an effective plan. The Gospel went to the world much faster than anyone thought was possible – anyone but Jesus, that is, who knew all along how well it was going to work when He set it all in motion.

Paul's epistles – follow up ministry to established churches – also give an indication of the extent of the worldwide church within that first generation. Galatia, Ephesus, Philippi, Colosse, Corinth, Rome, Thessalonica and Crete (Titus) – maturing churches spread across the Roman empire and beyond which give witness to the effectiveness of the plan implemented by the early church at Jesus' instigation. Since we use these epistles for guidance in our daily lives and ministry, we overlook the fact that they also record the spread of the Gospel in fulfillment of the great commission. The church was on the move.

Peter wrote to churches in Pontus, Galatia, Cappadocia, Asia and Bithynia, and sends greetings from the church in Babylon. James wrote to the "twelve tribes scattered abroad", obviously believers in churches throughout the region. Once again, we appreciate the wisdom and insight they share, but overlook the implications of church growth they also record.

By the end of that first generation of the church, when there was only one apostle left, much of the known world had heard the Gospel and was set to expand to the ends of the earth. That apostle, John, conveyed a message from the Head of the church to a whole other set of established churches, churches with ministries, influences and problems of their own. Ephesus, Smyrna, Pergamos, Thyatira, Sardis, Philadelphia, Laodicea – churches planted, blossoming and bringing forth fruit in more and more places across the Roman Empire.

Which brings up another point of interest – logistics. In an ancient world where safe travel would have been difficult, God had already planned and put in place the Roman Empire with its extensive roads and security systems, a mechanism for the effective transmission of the Gospel in that generation. Less than 300 years after the great commission was given, the church had spread to the far reaches of its world, supplanting polytheism and emperor worship as the official religion of the empire, worthy of the emperor Constantine himself. Who would have thought it? Only Jesus, Who understood it all along as He shepherded His church through its nascent days and into its illustrious future.

To lead the church into its long range future Jesus also had things put in writing – providing eye witness records through the Gospels and theological support through the epistles of Paul, Peter, James, John and Jude which later combined to form the written record which we know as the New Testament. And He has continually called people and gifted them for ministry to provide the framework for each generation to reach its world with the same unadulterated, un-diluted life-changing message of the gospel.

■ ■ ■

An organism which should have died, been killed or stamped out has, instead, taken root and flourished in a hostile environment, continually bringing the Gospel to hungry hearts and souls in every nation, people and culture. Down through the centuries, antagonistic rulers have tried to erase the church from their terri-tory, only to watch it thrive and grow under the worst conditions they can impose upon it. It's an amazing testimony to the effec-tiveness of the plan and the power, as witnessed by three recent examples.

One of the key tenets of the Soviet Union was the elimination of the church, "the opiate of the masses." For seventy years they oppressed, persecuted, imprisoned, and executed Christians. They razed churches and cathedrals, or turned them into museums or factories, and drove their congregations underground. They hunted down priests and pastors to decapitate the church, eliminating its leadership. And yet, it was the Soviet Union which collapsed while the church flourished, and today Russian leadership acknowledges that the church provides one of the most important foundational supports to their nation, without which they cannot face a difficult future.

When the communist Chinese drove the "foreign devil" mis-sionaries out of their country, the Chinese church numbered in the tens of thousands. Once again, the government set out to eliminate the church, actively pursuing, oppressing and persecuting Christians wherever they could find them. And yet, after a similar period of seventy years, the Chinese church numbers in the hundreds of millions and has begun sending missionaries into "needy" western nations. And the government is looking to Christians more and more to bring integrity into the new China.

And then there's the church in the good old US of A. Weakened by materialism and prosperity, the church still shares the Gospel, people are still finding the Lord, and missionaries are still being sent to far corners of the globe; because the plan compensates for all obstacles, and the power overcomes all weaknesses. And a young American, rejected by his home church and refused by mission boards, can still go off to a South American jungle and share the Gospel with the same results the first century church experienced.

■ ■ ■

The plan worked. The power was more than sufficient. Now the baton has been passed to us... Us, with our advanced technology. Us, with our advanced communications. Us, with our advanced travel capabilities. If they could reach their world, starting from scratch, surely we can reach ours, with all the resources we have at our disposal. Sure, the world population is now in the billions, but the church numbers in the millions.

It can be done. It must be done. The great commission is as valid today as it was then. They took it seriously, and with God's help they accomplished it. The plan has been effective for 2000 years. The power is still available, undiminished. Let's go. Our world is waiting.

Discussion questions:

1. What do we learn from how "a despised religion of outcasts and slaves could survive and thrive"?
2. How did planning for 2000 years alter the design of the plan?
3. How does the effectiveness of the plan encourage us today?
4. Summarize the plan and the power and the user's manual.
5. How do we know that the early church reached their world with the Gospel?
6. Give examples of the church's survival in tough situations.
7. What is the challenge for us today?

Made in the USA
Middletown, DE
12 August 2015